A Williamson *Little Hands*® Book

The essential hands-on guide to the new curriculum

KINDERGARTEN SUCCESS

Helping children excel right from the start

Jill Frankel Hauser

Illustrated by Savlan Hauser

WILLIAMSON BOOKS
NASHVILLE, TN

Library of Congress Cataloging-in-Publication Data

Hauser, Jill Frankel, 1950-
   Kindergarten success : helping children excel right from the start / Jill Frankel Hauser ; illustrated by Savlan Hauser.
      p. cm. — (A Williamson Little Hands book)
   Includes index.
   ISBN 0-8249-6758-5 (pbk. : alk. paper) — ISBN 0-8249-6777-1 (hardcover : alk. paper)
   1. Kindergarten—Activity programs—United States. I. Title. II. Series.
   LB1180.H38 2005
   372.21'8—dc22
                                        2005014257

Little Hands® series editor: **Susan Williamson**
Project editor: **Emily Stetson**
Interior design: **Sydney Wright**
Illustrations: **Savlan Hauser**
Cover design and cover illustrations: **Michael Kline**

Published by Williamson Books
An imprint of Ideals Publications
A division of Guideposts
535 Metroplex Drive, Suite 250
Nashville, Tennessee 37211
800-586-2572

Printed and bound in Italy
10 9 8 7 6 5 4 3 2 1

Books by Jill Frankel Hauser

(All are published by Williamson Books. Please see page 128 for ordering information)

EASY ART FUN!
Do-It-Yourself Crafts for Beginning Readers
A *Little Hands*® Read-&-Do book

Little Hands® **CELEBRATE AMERICA!**
Learning about the U.S.A. through Crafts & Activities

SCIENCE PLAY!
Beginning Discoveries for 2- to 6-Year-Olds

WOW! I'M READING!
Fun Activities to Make Reading Happen

GIZMOS & GADGETS
Creating Science Contraptions that Work (& Knowing Why)
A Williamson *Kids Can!*® book for ages 7 to 14, 144 pages

KIDS' CRAZY ART CONCOCTIONS
50 Mysterious Mixtures for Art & Craft Fun
A Williamson *Kids Can!*® book for ages 7 to 14, 160 pages

SUPER SCIENCE CONCOCTIONS
50 Mysterious Mixtures for Fabulous Fun
A Williamson *Kids Can!*® book for ages 7 to 14, 160 pages

Dedication

To my enthusiastic Rother School kindergartners for expanding my view of what young children can understand, create, and enjoy!

Acknowledgments

Janet Archey, Kari Gaspardone, Susan Schroth, and Barbara Zlotowski for your thoughtful review.

Contents

Success in the "New" Kindergarten

Peek into a kindergarten classroom, and you'll see young children reading books, writing in journals, and solving math problems. Today's five-year-olds experience a very different kindergarten than the one attended by their parents a generation ago. Learning goals, now known as *standards*, clearly lay out what these children must know to be successful in the challenging school years ahead.

The curriculum shaped by these standards is rigorous. Whereas kindergartners used to be taught basics such as recognizing colors and tying their shoes, it's now assumed that children begin school with these capabilities in place. Learning the alphabet and numbers were once year-end goals, but today's kindergartners apply alphabet knowledge to actual reading and writing, and they apply basic number sense to mathematical reasoning. Expectations are high!

Why Be Concerned About Kindergarten Success?

Acquiring the competencies a graduating high school student needs to succeed in college and in the global economy starts in kindergarten. Standards define the necessary foundation for achievement 12 years later. What children learn during one school year becomes the crucial building block for the next. **Research shows that children who get off to a good start maintain their advantage throughout their schooling. So meeting the standards in kindergarten is critical.**

Are five-year-olds prepared for the challenge? Traditional kindergarten programs waited for the child to be "ready" to learn. Today's successful kindergarten programs recognize that the sorts of experiences we offer children affect readiness. **Challenging learning experiences can actually *advance* the level of what a child is ready and able to learn.**

The Challenge: Creating a Vibrant Environment for Learning

So, must kindergarten now be dominated by drills, work sheets, and desk work? Not at all! As I train teachers across the country, they express this same concern: *How do we help young children meet the standards with activities that are still appropriate for the way they best learn?* In my own classroom, I've discovered that implementing high standards can actually present an opportunity to redesign kindergarten into a child-centered environment in which children develop their most vital learning tool — their own minds.

The activities in *Kindergarten Success* align with standards from each academic curricular area: Language and Literacy, Mathematics, Science, Social Studies, and the Arts. Learning is paramount while the joy, enthusiasm, and sense of wonder that are forever the heart and soul of kindergarten remain. The hands-on, minds-on activities are not only effective, but also respect the playful, exploratory way children learn best. When children are challenged to think creatively, examine critically, and problem-solve, they master the required standards ... and *much* more. They leave kindergarten knowing *how* to learn.

Yes, children must learn *basic skills* ("I know my ABCs") and understand *concepts* ("I understand that letters represent sounds"). But it is through *deeper thinking* that children apply skills and concepts in a meaningful way that cements their learning and builds independence. ("How do I read this book? I sound out the words and think about if they make sense! I use strategies to get at the meaning of the story.") **Self-directed learning begins when children apply what they've learned to new situations to attain their goals.** Instead of a bleak classroom dominated by rote learning, imagine the new kindergarten as a vibrant place where thinking prevails and children start to take charge of their own learning!

Parents Are Key

Standards are set at a demanding level that assumes parents will join in supporting children's learning. The good news is that children can meet standards comfortably — *if* they come from homes where daily outings are transformed into world experiences, language is rich, literacy experiences are shared, math happens as the table is set, and learning is valued. As a kindergarten teacher, I've observed that students who come to school ready to learn get so much more from classroom experiences. These kids are confident and are receptive to learning because of their readiness. **Sharing the activities in *Kindergarten Success* at home will give children the competence they need to succeed in the classroom ... and beyond!**

Mentors Make the Difference

Kindergarten Success uses both *guided exploration* and *guided instruction,* with a mentor playing a crucial role. We'll define mentor as an expert, someone more knowledgeable than the child. She could be a teacher, parent, older child, or peer.

Exploring the nature of things. One way children learn is through exploration guided by a mentor. What better way to find out how water behaves, for instance, than to explore it? In an activity designed by the mentor, children explore to build their own understanding of the physical world around them. Let kids pour water into a variety of bottles and they discover that water takes on the shape of its container. Let children play with blocks and they discover principles of stability. While petting a kitten, kids discover a furry body covering unlike their own skin. **Because children construct their own sense of their world through play, exploration, and experimentation, guided exploration is an ideal way to learn about the nature of things.**

Show me, guide me, let me do it on my own! Other types of learning require a different sort of focus. Exploring a two-wheeler, for example, is not the most effective way to learn how to ride it. "How-to" knowledge (how to ride a bike, swim, tie shoes, and, yes, read) is different from learning about the nature of things (that bubbles pop, balls roll downward, ice cream melts), and so it is acquired quite differently. Proficiency at a task is best learned from a mentor — an expert who shows you how.

Think about how you learned to ride a bike. First a mentor, maybe a parent, *modeled* how it's done: *See how I hold onto the handles, pedal hard, and balance?* Next, your mentor *guided* as she held the bike steady while you got on and pedaled. Then there was monitored, diminished support. She held on with both hands, then one hand on and one off, then she simply ran alongside. Finally, you were *on your own*, riding independently off into the sunset!

Through *guided instruction* (not lectures!), kindergartners learn how to read, write, and perform mathematical tasks. It's an interactive process that supports the child as she moves towards proficiency. **Through monitored support, the learner feels what it's like to be competent, long before she attains independence!**

Classic Learning 101

Mentor: **an expert who transfers mastery to the learner.**

Guided Exploration: **a model for learning about the nature of things.**
The mentor offers materials and activities for exploration that lead the learner to discover the characteristics of things.

Guided Instruction: **a model for how-to learning.**
Through the monitored support of a mentor, the learner gets a feel for proficiency long before he is skilled.
   "**Show me.**" The mentor *models* the skill.
   "**Guide me.**" The mentor and learner perform the skill together. The learner does as much as she can with the mentor filling in and *guiding* the learner along. Support is gradually diminished.
   "**Let me.**" The learner performs independently, *on her own.*

Building on What They Know

All children bring something special to kindergarten — themselves! Their own experiences are where learning begins. Children learn best when they build on what they already know. New knowledge must link to the familiar to be internalized. What better way to make knowledge accessible than through real-world tasks that connect to children's lives?

Opportunities for child-centered, authentic tasks abound at home: *How many forks do we need on the dinner table? Let's write the shopping list. This book explains how to care for our new kitten.* The classroom learning community is also rich with possibilities: *Let's make Dalaynee birthday cards. We need to make a sign that shows kids where to find the games. We can conduct a survey to figure out our favorite snack.* **When learning links to their lives, children come to appreciate knowledge.** *Kindergarten Success* shows parents and teachers how to seize these child-centered opportunities for making learning exciting and vital.

Connecting Throughout the Curriculum

Linking learning to kids' lives means connecting it in every possible way. *Kindergarten Success* weaves ideas, skills, and strategies throughout the curriculum. While studying seeds (SCIENCE), children write (LANGUAGE AND LITERACY) and draw (THE ARTS) their observations in a log. Children measure and record

There's the cereal!

CEREAL

the length of the sprouts (MATHEMATICS). **In the process, new knowledge is applied and integrated to deepen learning.**

Communicating Ideas

Sharing what you think and know is vital to learning. Talking, drawing, writing, diagramming, singing, and acting are some of the ways young children can share their observations, discoveries, and thinking. Ask key questions to inspire rich communication: *Why did you decide to do it that way? What do you predict will happen next? What did you discover? What do you make of it? What makes you think so?*

Through the process of communication, children organize their ideas and solidify their understanding. Communication also provides a clear window to kids' thinking. What a perfect way to assess and tailor the next learning experience to the meet the learner's needs! *Kindergarten Success* offers many ways for children to communicate as well as questions mentors can pose to help shape and assess learning.

Creating a Community of Learners

Today's kindergarten is a place where every child counts! Children explore together, share discoveries, and learn from one another. There is no one right answer when children are challenged to think creatively, examine critically, and problem-solve. All ways of thinking enrich the experience. And because a focus on deeper thinking fosters divergent thinking, the learning community is strengthened. Cooperation and respect are essential in a setting where learners are interdependent and diverse thinking is celebrated.

Beginning ... Now!

Which activity should I do first? When is the best time to introduce it? The simple answer is, any activity, anytime! Learning activities are loosely organized from simplest to most challenging within a chapter. For example, it's generally easier to sort objects (page 42) than to come up with an equation that defines an event (page 56). However, don't avoid talking about how many more apples we need to buy until kids have had a chance to sort and make patterns. Seize opportunities as they arise. Kids can write (the last activity in LANGUAGE AND LITERACY) long before they recognize letters when we honor their scribbles as first attempts. The child's level of interest will help you decide which activities to try and how much time to spend. Return to favorites again and again. Think *exposure*, *experience*, and *opportunity* rather than mastery.

I'll measure.

Making Everyday Connections

The more connected the learning, the more meaningful it is to the child and the better it is understood. Look here for ways to apply new learning across the curriculum in the classroom or throughout the day at home.

DEEPEN kids' understanding

These ideas challenge children to think critically and creatively. Children are offered rationale for *why* they are doing what they are doing and they are encouraged to be reflective. Suggestions are also given for *thinking aloud* (see below). Promoting deeper understanding rather than rote memorization gives kids the capability to apply new skills and strategies to novel situations — the ultimate goal of learning.

Think Aloud

"Thinking aloud" is a powerful instructional strategy. It sheds light on a thinking process that is often mysterious to young learners. For example, a mentor (indicated by italic type throughout the book) might help children better comprehend text by sharing her own thinking: *You know what good readers do to better understand a story? They see pictures in their heads as they read. Sort of like a movie. So as I'm reading this part, I can imagine the frog, sitting so still, just waiting for a fly to come by. Then, zap, he gets it with his long, sticky tongue!* The thinking process, ordinarily invisible, is made apparent and accessible to the child.

Children can think aloud, too. Possible child responses in *Kindergarten Success* are indicated by quotation marks: "I know how to write the word! I make each sound: /d/ /i/ /n/ /o/. And then I write down the letters: **d i n o**." Thinking aloud helps children crystallize concepts so that they can apply what they've learned on their own.

Get Involved!

Kindergarten Success is a guide for teachers, parents, caregivers, youth-group leaders, librarians — anyone who cares about young children and wishes to create a vibrant learning environment that makes kids' capabilities and enthusiasm for learning soar.

Jill Hauser

Language AND Literacy

Discovering the power of communication

Children come to school with wonderful language and literacy experiences teachers can build on. Parent response to babbling starts children communicating. Putting words to kids' experiences develops understanding, language, and vocabulary. Noticing print on the cereal box, listening to books read aloud, and joining in on an e-mail to Grandma are vital first steps toward literacy. Kindergartners are motivated to listen, speak, read, and write when the purpose continues to be meaningful communication.

Because written language is built on *oral language* and an *alphabetic system*, these are areas of major focus in kindergarten. But even as children learn the basics of letter names and sounds, communication — not rote memorization — must be the heart of any kindergarten literacy program.

The activities here build mastery of language and literacy by capitalizing on a kindergartner's natural desire to communicate. By treating skills as ways for gleaning and expressing ideas, children come to see language and literacy as powerful tools for enriching their lives and attaining their goals!

It's Standard!

Kindergarten language and literacy content includes:

* Vocabulary and language development
* Print concepts
* Alphabet knowledge
* Phonemic awareness
* Phonics and word recognition
* Fluency
* Comprehension
* Writing

Talk About It

Language and vocabulary are the tip of the iceberg. What lies beneath? Rich experiences, that's what. Without the experiences they stand for, words are meaningless. *Word* knowledge is built through *world* knowledge —

experiences at the beach as well as in the bathtub. Just be sure to add language!

Rich language strengthens a child's ability to communicate. It also shapes thinking. When my kindergartners contrast bare *deciduous* trees with green-needled *evergreens* on a fall walk, they realize that nature can be organized in an exciting new way. And, because command of spoken language sets the ceiling for understanding text, their comprehension of the books we read about trees is deepened.

Most language is learned indirectly, so immerse kindergartners in rich language all day! Harvest vocabulary from meaningful experiences and great read-aloud books, too.

Language Immersion

Every experience is a language-learning opportunity. Seize them all!
In a grocery store . . .

Model. Think aloud through rich speech. *Which melon shall we buy? This one smells fragrant. Let's purchase it for dessert.*

Guide. Extend children's words. When a child says "that one" add to the thought: *Oh, you want the cantaloupe. It's the heavy, orange-colored fruit with the rough skin. I think it's ripe because this end is soft and it smells so sweet.*

On their own. Encourage self-expression. *So what do you think of the melon? How does it taste?*

Delicious melon!

Harvest Rich Words

Read-aloud picture books provide a wonderful source for new vocabulary words.

Choose. Pick a word that is both critical to the understanding of the story and useful to the child in a variety of situations: **immense**

> The elephant laughed.
> "Why of all silly things!
> I haven't feathers and I haven't wings.
> ME on your egg? Why, that doesn't make sense. . . .
> Your egg is so small, ma'am, and I'm so **immense**."
> From *Horton Hatches the Egg* by Dr. Seuss

Clues. Think aloud to model how to figure out word meaning from context clues. *Your egg is so* **small**, *and I'm so* **immense** *. . . Hmmm . . . I know what small means. Horton sure isn't small. He's huge, the opposite of small.*

Muse. Come up with a kid-friendly definition: *So* **immense** *must mean "huge."*

Use. Guide children in using the word in a new context. *Those burgers at lunch today were immense. Could you kids finish them?*

A bee is small. A dinosaur is immense.

*Now you try it:
A _____ is small. A _____ is immense. Draw a picture of your idea.* The more engaged kids are with a word, the more likely they are to remember it and use it. That's the ultimate goal!

Transform the ordinary into the EXTRAordinary!

Substitute rich words for the common words kids hear repeatedly. By simply upgrading the language of our daily routines, I've been amazed by my kindergartners' eloquent speech!

✳ *It's lunchtime — I'm* **famished**.
✳ **Load** *your backpack.*
✳ **Vacate** *the classroom*
✳ **Fascinating!**

Don't **obliterate** your block tower!

DEEPEN kids' understanding

I find that the more "anchors" I provide for the target word, the better the children's understanding and the more likely they are to use the word. So I pick one or two of these word anchors for my students to talk about, draw, or act out. To be sure new words stick, we use them in as many situations as possible throughout the day. *Don't be* **glum** *because it's raining. Aren't you* **delighted** *Ethan is coming by?*

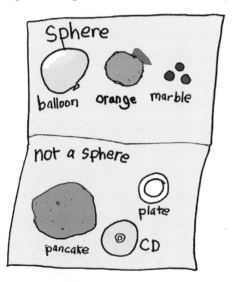

Anchors for the word *sphere:*

Category (what it is): *It's a 3-D shape.*

Examples: *ball, bubble, globe, marble, Tootsie Roll Pop*

Definition: *A* **sphere** *is a round shape like a ball.*

Funny visual: *I fear that sphere rolling toward me!*

Anchors for the word *delighted:*

It's like: *jubilant, joyous, happy, merry*

What it's not like: *miserable, sad, downhearted, glum*

See it: *The word on this page is* **delighted**. *Read it with me. Spell the word,* **d e l i g h t e d**. *Hear the /d/ sound?*

Making Everyday Connections

Language grows from experiences, so build vocabulary throughout the curriculum and at home.

Mathematics: most, least, more than, equal, heavier, shorter

Science: root, talons, fur, mammal, sand, cloud, evaporate

Social Studies: flag, symbol, community, justice, responsibility

Cooking: measure, mix, spatula, whisk, ingredients, tablespoon

I'll measure.

Print Has Something to Say

It's everywhere! Print is on signs, computer screens, food wrappers, and more. Help children understand that the *purpose* of those cool squiggles is to communicate ideas by focusing on the words in stories that delight them, packaging of food they love, and the most important word of all — *their names!*

Name Fame

My kindergartners start learning about print with the word most charged with meaning — their own names. Offer authentic opportunities to write signatures on greeting cards, artwork, and labels for possessions.

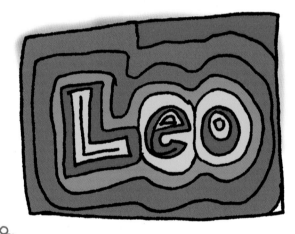

Rainbow Writing. Children trace around the letters of their names, each time using a different marker color. A colorful rainbow name and plenty of writing practice result!

Name Puzzle. Kids draw a picture of themselves on a large index card, then write their name beneath it, spacing out the letters. Cut between each letter (or groups of letters for a longer name) and through the picture to make puzzle pieces. Now, put the puzzle back together!

Note: A young child's signature may be only a distinctive scribble or simply a first letter. Remember to honor all first writing attempts!

Touch and Read

Model how to read:

- **Track** the print with your finger as you read, touching each word. Explain how there are spaces between words (see THE IMPORTANCE OF NOTHING, page 17). Explain how you follow words from left to right and from top to bottom on the page. Be explicit about how print works!

- **Point out** the front cover, back cover, spine, title page, table of contents, title, author, and illustrator of a book.

- **Frame,** using a WORD CATCHER (right): one letter, two letters, one word, two words, an uppercase letter, a lowercase letter, the first and last letters of words.

Then *guide* children how to read print as they track, point out, and frame along with you. Finally, have kids track, point out, and frame **on their own** when asked to show what they know.

Create a Word Catcher! Make this gizmo by cutting the jagged interior from two bread-bag tags. Hold one in each hand to frame a word.

Making Everyday Connections

Pretend with Print!

Print is a vital part of the adult world children love to imitate. When I add print props to my dramatic play center, kids instantly get busy reading and writing.

Restaurant: menus, cookbook, order pads, play money.

Travel agency, airport, bus or train station: tickets, schedules, brochures, postcards, travel posters, play money, luggage tags, travel magazines, guidebooks.

Health clinic, dental center, veterinary hospital: health brochures, invoices, clipboard, pencils, appointment cards, calendar, magazines and books for the waiting room.

The Importance of Nothing

No wonder beginning writing looks like a long string of letters. Don't we speak without pausing between words? Beginning readers don't realize that spaces mark boundaries between printed words. When my students "get it," this marks a huge leap in their literacy development. They are able to distinguish words from letters, accurately track read-aloud print, and leave spaces between words as they write!

Letter or Word? Kids use a ballpoint pen on enlarged text to circle letter after letter while chanting, "letter, letter, letter . . ." Next, they use a different-colored pen to circle words, noting spaces, while chanting, "word, word, word, . . ."

Make a Spacer. Trace the hand on this page onto a plastic milk jug. Cut it out. Kids can place this gizmo after each word to help them remember to leave spaces between words as they write. Use the spacer when you model writing as well.

DEEPEN kids' understanding

Our playground is in the shadow of the Golden Arches, so I was astonished that my students hadn't recognized the symbol as the letter **M**. Kids simply "logo-ize" print unless we bring it to their attention that these are meaningful letters and words.

Think aloud to model for kids how to go beyond logos to real reading: *That word starts with letter **b** . . . /b/ /b/ Burger King. So it can't be McDonald's!*

Make a Brand-Name Game Collect two examples of eight favorite brand names from packaging or advertisements. Paste each onto an index card. Use these cards to play a memory matching game.

I Own the Alphabet!

"Owning the alphabet" means knowing letter names, sounds, and how to write them. But the most important thing to know is that letters form words . . . words that can tell about all sorts of wonderful things!

Learning Letters: Six Easy Steps

1. Start with familiar language: *Listen for the letter **C** sound, /c/, as I read this story* (or *sing this song, say these names . . .*)

Snacks: carrots, cookies, cupcakes

A story: *The Berenstains' B Book* — letter **b**

A song or rhyme: "Jack and Jill" — letter **j**

Enviro-print: M&M's — letter **m**

Names: Nicole, Nicholas, Nathan — letter **n**

2. Listen to object word labels.
Pull items from a LETTER-SOUND BAG (shown). Emphasize the first letter sound as you say each object word. *Listen to these words. Hear how they all start with that same sound /c/: cookie, car, crayon, cat? What's the sound that starts these words? Yes, it's /c/.*

3. Look at and say picture word labels.
Show pictures from a labeled PICTURE BANK (purchase alphabet picture flash cards or create your own by pasting magazine pictures on index cards and writing the word beneath). *Let's say these picture words together. Listen for that same sound. What's the sound that starts these words? Yes, it's /c/. Look at the word labels. What do you notice? Yes, they start with the same letter, **c**.*

4. Practice letter writing. *Watch me spell (write) the sound. You form it along with me on the rug, your hand, in the air.*

5. Reinforce learning by making a book.
*Now let's make a letter **c** book. Fold two sheets of paper in half and staple them at the fold. Title your book "My Letter C Book." Then write the letter **c** many times on the first page. Draw a picture and write the word for things that start with letter **c** on each page.* Kids can use picture/word cards from the PICTURE BANK (step 3) for support.

6. Apply learning by reading words.
No need to wait for kids to learn every letter before beginning to read! As soon as they've learned three letters such as **a, c, t,** they are ready to read their first word, **cat**. As each new letter is learned, instantly apply the new knowledge to reading more words, such as **mat, man, can, jam** (see THE AH-HA! MOMENT OF READING, page 27).

Making Everyday Connections

Letters Alive!

Children who can name letters with confidence tend to make an easier transition to reading. It's easy to make connections to the alphabet throughout the day because letters are *everywhere!* Point out letters wherever you see them: on street signs, in advertising, in functional print. Kids love doing this. *Do you see those letters? Let's say them together.* Have kids watch for a target letter in a read-aloud book or in print around the home or classroom. Talk about letters that spell friends' names and brand names.

Making Sense of the Alphabet

It's no small task to learn 26 letter names. Use all the senses in vivid ways to increase learning!

🔖 *Feel* them

Bendables. Kids bend a pipe cleaner or two into each letter as they sing the ABCs.

Handfuls. Form each letter using the fingers of both hands!

Rub-a-dub. Write letters on cards with puffy fabric paint. Children place a sheet of paper on top to make letter rubbings.

The clay way. Press a thin layer of modeling clay into a large plastic lid. Kids use an old ballpoint pen to form letters in the clay, then rub the clay smooth with their fingers and try some more!

🔖 *Hear* them

Letter talk. Friends, family, and classmates take on new names when it's **w** day: Walisha, Wick, and Wason!

Sing a song. Once kids master the "ABC Song," sing it backward or with letter sounds while kids point to the letters on an alphabet chart.

Stepping-stones. Make chalk letter stepping-stones on the sidewalk. Kids sing the ABCs as they hop from letter to letter.

See them

Font fun. Gather letters in all sorts of fonts. Cut them from magazines. Print them from a computer and cut them out. Sort and say the letter names or sounds.

Read them. Enjoy alphabet books galore! Here are a few favorites: *Can you see the letter in each photograph of* Arlene Alda's ABC? *Watch letters transform in* Alphabatics *by Suse MacDonald.*

Collage. Write a letter in the center of a sheet of paper, then cut out or draw pictures that start with the same sound and paste them all around.

Looks like. Use a marker to write a large target letter on a sheet of paper. Use crayons to make the letter look like something that starts with that sound. An **m** can be transformed into a mountain, and an **o** into an octopus!

Taste and Smell them

Sort. Sort alphabet cereal, and then eat the piles as you say the letter name.

Squirt. Anything that squirts from a squeeze bottle makes a yummy letter: catsup, mustard, margarine, whipped cream, jam, or Cheese Whiz.

Bake. Form refrigerator cookie dough into letter shapes.

Cracking the Code

The magic of figuring out a printed word happens when children understand *phonics* — the link between language sounds and letter symbols. They bring to the task their knowledge of print, the alphabet, and one other key understanding called *phonemic awareness*. This awareness of the small sound units that make up our speech dramatically increases reading success.

Why is phonemic awareness so critical? It's because our alphabet matches speech to print at the smallest unit, or *phoneme*. If children lack this understanding, the alphabetic code is illogical. What a challenge for beginners! Since birth kids have been listening to speech for meaning. A **cat** is that wonderful, furry critter you love that purrs on your lap and licks you. It's not a /c/ /a/ /t/! But children must make the shift from listening for *meaning* to listening for *sounds* in order to become readers.

Once they have an awareness of sounds within spoken words and knowledge of the sounds each alphabet symbol represents, children are prepared to decode words they see in print — a giant step toward independent reading and writing!

Literacy Lingo

alphabetic principle: Each spoken phoneme is represented by a written letter spelling. Change a letter, change a word.

c-v-c words: consonant-vowel-consonant words (**red, bat, hog**).

decode: reading a word by figuring out its symbol-to-sound relationships.

encode: writing a word by figuring out its sound-to-symbol relationships.

fluency: effortless reading that sounds like talk.

high-frequency words: words that appear most often in print (**the, a, is**).

onset: first consonant(s) sound of a syllable (**sl**-ip, **b**-ug).

phoneme: the smallest sound unit of speech (/m/).

phonemic awareness: the ability to identify and play with phonemes.

phonics: the system of phonemes and the letter spellings that represent them.

rime: part of the syllable starting with the vowel and the letters that follow (sl-**ip**, b-**ug**).

syllable: a word part containing a vowel (but-ter).

Rhyme Time

Children's natural attraction to rhyme makes it an excellent way to spark phonemic awareness. Listening to rhymes helps children tune into the similarities and differences in sounds within words, and discover patterns in word structure (r**at**, b**at**, m**at** . . .).

Finish That Thought

From nursery rhymes to Dr. Seuss to Raffi songs, wonderful rhyming language to share abounds. Say a couplet with the last word missing. Encourage children to use rhyme to figure out what the word could be.

Rhyme Hunt.

Paste a picture of an object on a bag, say a shoe. Ask children to find things, draw pictures, or cut out magazine photos to rhyme with the target word. How about a jar of **glue** or picture of **stew**? Why put a cow in the bag? It says, "Moo!" Note that it doesn't matter how words are spelled, only how they *sound*.

Gather bags for several rhyming word families. Now dump out the bags so that all the words are mixed up. *Can you sort them back into the correct groups?*

It's a Rhyme Storm!

Pick a word such as **man**. *How many rhyming words can we brainstorm?* "Fan, can, pan, ran!" Nonsense words are fine, too: "zan, tran, gan!" Pick a new word when you are all rhymed out!

fan

can

pan

Alliteration Celebration

The first sound of a word is the easiest phoneme for children to hear. The alphabet activities (pages 18–21) also target alliteration and the first sounds in words.

Sounds Like Me! The sound that starts a child's name is extra-special. Here, children create books of sounds that match their names!

MATERIALS: 2 sheets of paper, stapler, markers and crayons, scissors, magazines, paste, highlighter pen

1. Fold two sheets of paper in half. Staple along the fold. Let each child draw his picture and write his name on the cover.

2. On each inside page, draw or paste a picture to match the sound of the first letter of his name (Jordan may draw a jeep, jet, or even paste in a Jell-O advertisement).

3. Help children write words to label the pictures. Now, help them read their books, emphasizing the first letter sound. Together, use a highlighter pen to identify the first letter of each word. *Look! All the words start with the same sound **and** the same letter!*

Game Time. Use the format of the rhyming games to focus on first-letter sounds. Play SOUND HUNT by having children search for objects that start with the sound that starts the word for the picture on a LETTER-SOUND BAG (page 18). Play SOUND STORM by brainstorming words that start with the same sound as the chosen word (**banana: button, boat, bracelet, barrette**, . . .).

Blend and Split

Build awareness of words, syllables, and phonemes as unique language sound units with these games. Phonemes present the greatest challenge. A beginning reader may correctly say /h/ /e/ /n/ when encountering the word **hen** in print but *think* the word is **hat**. Reading requires blending phonemes into the word. Writing requires the same skill in reverse: splitting the word into phonemes and writing letter symbols to match each one.

Word Wise. Clap for each *word* in a sentence. Start simply: *I love you. That's three!* Now talk about how **I love pizza** is still a three-clap sentence. Words are sound units that have meaning.

Syllable Speak. Use a hand puppet (see PUPPET PLAY, page 118) to test for syllables in names of friends. Count how many times the puppet closes its mouth to say a name. *Han-nah, that's two. Nich-o-las, that's three.* Test everyday objects and sort them into piles of one-, two-, three-syllable (or more) words. My students become so adept, I can simply clap one or more times to dismiss them by the number of syllables in their names!

Han-nah

Penny Push-Ups. Place three circle stickers side by side on an index card. Put a penny beneath each circle. Children slide a penny onto a circle for each sound heard in a word. Think *sounds*, not letters. These words, for example, each have three sounds: /p/ /e/ /n/, sh/ /o/ /p/, m/ /oo/ /n/

Make a two-circle card for words like **shoe, up,** and **go.** Make a four-circle card for words like **fast, plane,** and **frog.**

Sing It! Practice sound blending to the tune of "The Wheels on the Bus."

The sounds in my word say

/j/ /e/ /t/, /j/ /e/ /t/, /j/ /e/ /t/,

The sounds in my word say /j/ /e/ /t/,

Can you guess my word?

Jet!

sound POWER

Fun language games, songs, and activities give children critical insight into speech.

Keep it fun and fast. Just a few minutes a day goes a long way.

Practice phonemic awareness on the go. Your voices are all that's needed. In a classroom, use these activities during transition time, while lining up or settling down.

Add letters that match target sounds whenever possible. Place a letter card in each pile when sorting items from LETTER-SOUND BAGS (page 18).

The larger and more meaningful the sound chunk, the easier it is to hear. Start by pointing out *sentences* as super-short stories. Then focus on meaningful *words*, such as children's names or object and action labels. Next, play sound games to help children notice abstract *syllables* and *phonemes*.

The Ah-ha! Moment of Reading

After learning just enough letters to form a word (**a, c, t**), follow these steps with a child to figure out all "sound out" words.

Model. *Listen while I blend these sounds together to read a word. I put my finger under each letter and say the sound each makes. Then I put my finger back to the beginning of the word. I sweep through while blending the sounds to say the word.*

Guide. *Place your finger on top of mine and try it with me.*

On their own. *Now, use your finger to try it by yourself. WOW, you're really reading!*

Actual reading is the best, most complete literacy experience. As kids track print on the page with their fingers, they practice *print concepts*. As they say sounds for each letter symbol, they strengthen *alphabet* ownership and *phonics* skills. As they blend those sounds together, they practice *phonemic awareness*. Best of all, through reading they experience the rationale for learning all those tricky, abstract, requisite skills — discovering meaning from print! Ah-ha!

Note: Now children need little books they can really read to keep up the momentum and support their budding skills! These series use words beginners can decode: Bob Books for Beginning Readers by Bobby Lynn Maslen (Scholastic); Now I'm Reading for Beginning Readers (Innovative Kids); and Step Into Reading: Phonics First Steps! by Ron Lieser (Random House). Brand New Readers (Candlewick Press) uses predictable sentence patterns to propel beginners through the text.

Word-Family Play

Word-family play rapidly grows a child's bank of "sound out" words. Children come to understand the *alphabetic principle* (change a letter, change a word) when they physically manipulate letters and word chunks.

It's more efficient to sound /p/ /ig/ (onset and rime) instead of /p/ /i/ /g/ (each phoneme). To encourage my students to sound out words this way and to help them see the pattern within a word family, we sing this song to the tune of "Here We Go 'Round the Mulberry Bush."

If I can spell **pig**, /p/ /ig/
Then I can spell **wig**, /w/ /ig/
And I can spell **fig**, /f/ /ig/
/ig/ stays the same, **i g**!

(continue down a list of **-ig** words)

Flip Book Fun. Use an index card as a base. Write the rime to the right. Staple a stack of onset strips to the left of the rime. Kids flip through the stack to create and read words.

Slick Word Slider. Cut parallel slits on the left side of index cards. Weave a strip of onset letters through. Write the rime on the right side of the cards. Kids slide the strip through the windows to create and read words.

Word Builder. Cut index cards into thirds. Write onset letters on each piece. Write the rime on the left side of 10 other index cards. Kids can build words by matching onsets to rimes. Teachers can use a pocket chart to make this a class activity. Parents can have kids build words at the table. Challenge kids to write and record the list of words they build.

What about "the"?

One hundred simple words make up about half of the words in print. Many cannot be sounded out. Being able to read these *high-frequency words* quickly and accurately builds fluency. Kindergartners can begin to learn some of these important words for reading and writing such as:

the and to we he she you a I my see can like it is

Catch That Word! Use a WORD CATCHER (page 16) to frame a high-frequency word for a quick response. Or, slide the frame open, revealing each letter in sequence for sounding out words.

Find it: Ask the child to use the word catcher to frame the target word wherever it appears in the text. *Can you find . . .?*

Read it: Frame random words for the child to read. *Can you read this word?*

Crash, Boom! Set a stack of high-frequency word cards in front of one or two kids. Mix in a **boom** card and a **crash** card. Kids take turns reading and keeping cards from the stack. **Boom** means take another turn. **Crash**, and you have to give a card back.

Fluency Fun

Fluency is the hallmark of capable readers. Beginners plod through text because they must focus on decoding every word. Little mental energy is left for understanding. Through lots of literacy experiences, children are able to read words *automatically* and *accurately*. Eventually, reading aloud sounds natural, like speech. When readers read with *expression*, they are reading efficiently, identifying words and comprehending at the same time.

Can beginners experience fluency? Yes! Give kids many opportunities to hear fluent models:

You! Read aloud to children, daily. Track the print with your finger as you read. Now give the child a chance to try with simple text.

Recorded stories. Books that come with a tape or CD allow children to hear expressive reading. Encourage them to read along.

Recorded songs. Make a song sheet by printing the lyrics for favorite melodies. Familiar songs model the wonderful rhythm of language while supporting kids as they track and read the print.

DEEPEN kids' understanding

Sometimes I hold up a flash card to my kindergartners and say, *Don't read this word. Tell me **how** to read the word.* I make the decoding strategy accessible to them by teaching this song to the tune of "London Bridge."

Every letter has a sound
Say each sound
Blend aloud
Listen to the sounds you heard
What's the word?

Making Everyday Connections

Explore a rime family from a familiar, authentic context: *Look for the -at chunk as I read this story* (or *sing this song, say these names …*).

A story (*The Three Little Pigs* for -ig)

A song or rhyme ("Jack and Jill" for -ack, -ill)

Enviro-print (Kit-Kat bar for -at, -it)

Names (Jordan, Antoinette for -an).

Now I Get It!

Understanding is the very reason for reading. Skilled readers build understanding by *thinking actively* as they read. Because a beginning reader's listening level far exceeds her reading ability, we teach kindergartners to apply these valuable thinking strategies to text that is read *to* them. The prize? A glorious world of knowledge and stories!

Building Understanding

Different kinds of questions invite different kinds of thinking. I have found that *meaning* and *beyond* questions challenge my students to think deeply. They interact with one another in a lively "grand conversation" that promotes a love of reading.

Recall. Guide kids to restate the information: *Who tried to blow the pig's house down? What color is the frog?*

Get at deeper meanings. Children take what the author says and combine it with their own knowledge to construct a deeper understanding. *Which pig was the smartest? How does green coloring help the frog?*

Extend. Go beyond the story to make judgments or inspire new ideas: *Was it right to trick the wolf?* Or, to be creative: *Design your own critter. What features does it have for protection?*

Who Is Your Sunshine?

All text is fair game for practicing comprehension strategies and grappling with meaning, even song lyrics! Explore the lyrics to the chorus of "You Are My Sunshine" by Jimmie Davis.

You are my sunshine, my only sunshine,
You make me happy when skies are gray,
You'll never know, dear, how much I love you,
So please don't take my sunshine away.

Kindergartners can **infer meaning** ("So, when skies are gray must mean when times are tough. My sunshine is a special someone I love."), **identify the central idea** ("Someone I love can make me happy, even when I'm sad."), **make a connection to the text** ("My sunshine is my sister because she plays with me!"), and **visualize** ("I'll paint her picture!"). **Skilled readers use strategies flexibly and in combination. So can kindergartners!**

Jose is my sunshine because he plays with me.

 ## My Special Sunshine

MATERIALS: plate, marker, art paper, watercolors, paintbrush

1. Trace around a plate with a marker to make a large sunshine circle at the center of the art paper.

2. Have children paint their special someone inside the circle and sun rays outside the circle. Let paint dry.

3. Have children write across the bottom of their painting: _____ is my sunshine because _____.

Strategy Savvy

Research shows that teaching comprehension strategies improves understanding. You'll need rich text to support this deeper thinking. Don't "over-strategize" a fun read-aloud experience. Just pick the one or few best suited to the material.

What's next? Make predictions while reading to propel kids through the text.

Let's find out. Set a purpose before reading a book.

Mind's eye. Create mental images while reading.

Connections. Link reading to life, the world, and other texts.

Text structure. Identify characters, setting, events, solutions, big ideas, details . . .

Key ideas. Discover main ideas and themes.

Graphic organizers. Process information visually.

Monitoring. Know and correct when understanding falls apart.

DEEPEN kids' understanding

When I introduce a new comprehension strategy to my students, I let them in on what goes on in my head. I *think aloud* to explicitly model how to use the strategy. Then I ask questions to support them in using it on their own. Soon I hear little voices chiming in during a new read-aloud: "That part of the story reminds me of when my brother broke his promise. I was really mad!"

Model. Good readers make connections to the story as they read. **The Little Engine That Could** *reminds me of the time I thought I couldn't skate. I fell down a lot, but I kept on trying. Now I love inline skating!*

Guide. Can you think of a time you thought something would be hard to do, but you kept on trying, and now you can?

On their own. During a new story ask kids, *What does this remind you of?*

I think I can ... and I can!

"But I don't get it!"

What do good readers do when understanding falls apart? Most important, they are aware when they're not getting it. We've all had the experience of reading text, then realizing we can't remember a thing we've read. Good readers stop, slow down, and read it again.

Ask kids to listen for something fascinating in what you are about to read. Read a short passage. Then ask kids to turn to each other, or you, and share, "It's fascinating that …" or "I didn't know that …" Read the passage again if kids can't think of anything.

Making Everyday Connections

Think of what you read on a typical day: e-mail, newspapers, catalogs, how-to guides, reference material, and if you're lucky you can fit in the novel on your nightstand! Be sure to include informational text read-alouds: topics of interest like snakes, volcanoes, and firefighting; how-to books like making crafts, concocting science experiments, or cooking. Deepen kids' understanding of these materials by using the questioning and strategies presented here.

The Write Start

Writing is the pinnacle of literacy. Here's where children apply all requisite skills. Given *learning experiences* and the *language* to describe them, kids have important ideas to express. Because they know about *print concepts*, they write from left to right, top to bottom, and make spaces between their words. *Phonemic awareness* helps them split apart the sounds of the words they want to write. Ownership of the *alphabet* lets them match those sounds to letters. Now they can *phonetically* spell any word they like. While **dinosr** isn't conventional spelling, it is sensible spelling that communicates. With so much literacy knowledge, it's no wonder kindergartners can write mini-essays on topics they study in school!

Sentence Starters

Sentence starters support beginning writers. Kids can copy the starter, then fill in the rest by sounding out the words or copying the words from labeled picture flash cards. Kids can create My Books (page 37) filled with a particular starter, such as *I Can by Madison.*

I see a	**I can**
See my	**My**
I like my	**The**
I like to	**I am**

Note: Sentence starters support beginners. As soon as kids are able to go beyond and write about their own ideas, phase out sentence starters. Remember, the purpose of writing is to communicate ideas.

Celebrate Writing!

Writing evolves from scribbles to pictures to letter-like squiggles and letter chains. Next you'll notice "sensible spellings" where kids apply emerging letter sound knowledge by phonetically spell **lzr** for **lizard** or **jrk** or **jrec** for **drink.** Children's writing becomes increasingly more conventional with lots of writing and reading experiences plus your modeling, guidance, and feedback. So, celebrate those first scribbles by asking kids to "read" their messages to you. Your enthusiastic response reinforces the reason for writing — communication! Kids come to understand the power of print when they create written messages of their own. Let their writing flow!

Scribble Writing

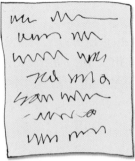

A shopping list.

Drawings and Strings of Letters

SPTOMINLO

"I like pizza."

Phonetic Writing

Elfns jrec wif vr trux.

"Elephants drink with their trunks."

Conventional Writing

Dear Ashley,
Let's play jumprope.
Love,
Liz ♥

My Office. Stock a writing center with tools of the trade: pads of paper, sheets of lined, colored, and blank paper, stationery, envelopes, index cards, alphabet stencils, safety scissors, gummed stamps, rubber stamps, staples, tape, glue stick, paper clips ... and let the writing begin!

My Mail. Have kids decorate an empty tissue box as the perfect place for receiving messages, postcards, and greeting cards from classmates or family members.

My Books. Show kids how two folded sheets of paper stapled at the spine make a book. Anyone can be an author!

Pen Pals

Interactive writing is a hands-on way to give kids access to the writing process. The pen moves back and forth from child to child or child to mentor, with the mentor filling in the knowledge the children lack. The mentor thinks aloud and delivers on-the-spot mini-lessons that show kids exactly how to transform spoken words into print.

Decide on a message to work with, such as **I love black cats.** Then share every step of the process.

1. **First word.** *How do we know what word to write first? Let's say the message again slowly and listen for what comes first. It's **I**! Who can write **I**?* A child writes "I" on a marker board or large sheet of paper for all to see in a classroom, or on a sheet of paper at home.

2. **Spacing.** *What must we do after writing a word? Jason can mark the space with his hand.*

3. **How do I know what to write next?** *I go back to the beginning and touch and read the words I've written so far. That helps me remember. **I** ... yes, the next word is **love**.*

4. **Words we know.** *Jackie always writes **love**. She'll write it for us here. Or: Let's copy **love** from our Word List.*

5. **Phonetic words.** *How can we figure out how to spell **black**? Yes, let's split apart the sounds. Can you write letters for those sounds? You're right! Let's split apart the sounds in **cats** the same way.*

6. **Edit.** *Are we finished? No. We must check our writing. Let's go back to the beginning and touch and read. Do our voice words match our written words? Did we start with an uppercase letter? Did we leave spaces between words? Do we have a period at the end? Uh-oh. Let's add one now!*

What do I **write** about?

Kids can write only what they can say. Always have kids talk about the topic or their idea as the planning stage for writing. Inspire kindergartners to write with these fun prompts.

* **All I know** about a topic (bugs, frogs, weather, sports . . .)
* **What I'm expert at** (soccer, tumbling, cat care . . .)
* **How to** (make a sandwich, make a simple craft, play tic-tac-toe . . .)
* **Alternative endings** to stories
* **Favorites** (toys, books, pets . . .)
* **Descriptions** (time of day, clothing, a friend . . .)
* **Dreams** (I wish, If ...)
* **Issues** (I think we need more playgrounds because . . .)

"First get peanut butter."

⟲DEEPEN kids' understanding

While writing seems easy for us, it's a huge, new concept for many children. Interactive writing has proved to be a wonderful way to show how writing works in my classroom. Rather than telling kids what to write, I ask questions that empower them with the strategy. So instead of saying, *Now write the word* *bug*, I ask, *How do we figure out what word to write next?* This is a challenging question for someone who has never put her words on paper! As children grapple with the process, it soon becomes their own. The time spent guiding is well worth the effort when the children blossom into independent writers!

Making Everyday Connections

Kids *CAN!*

Writing is like thinking. It can happen all the time, anywhere. Encourage children to write, and explain to them what writing is about, whenever you can! With your support, kids can:

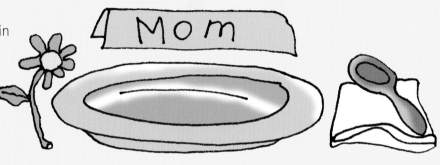

✳ Write (and read with help) greeting cards and letters.

✳ Make name cards for guests.

✳ Create "word hugs" for friends.

✳ Help with shopping lists.

✳ Read safety and reminder signs.

✳ Make organizational labels.

✳ Read book reviews.

✳ Make brochures about our town (page 97).

✳ Interview older friends or family members (page 93).

Note: Before thinking kindergartners *can't*, remember the stages of writing (page 37). A book review kindergarten-style might be a picture of a favorite part of the story. The message in a greeting card could be scribbles or copied words. A town brochure might show drawings of great spots. Kindergartners *can* . . . when we honor their writing — at every level — as the communication it truly is!

Mathematics

From basic skills to problem solving

Mathematics is a way of thinking and communicating. It's part of the human experience, from fast-food purchases to voyages through space. It offers explanations for who has the most crayons as well as how the universe works. In kindergarten, children explore the same key concepts that are the mathematical basis for rocket science!

The three integrated levels of learning math are *basic skills* ("I can count"), *conceptual understandings* ("I understand that I can count objects in any order, just so long as each is accounted for, once"), and *problem solving* ("I can apply my counting skill to be sure we all get the same number of jelly beans"). When children use their skills and understandings to solve problems in kindergarten, they begin to see mathematics as a valuable tool for finding solutions to problems in their daily lives.

The activities in this section build mastery of math content. At the same time, children are guided to observe, make connections, question, think logically, and ultimately become powerful lifelong problems solvers!

It's Standard!

Kindergarten math content includes:

* Sorting and classifying
* Patterns
* Number sense
* Simple addition and subtraction
* Geometry
* Measurement
* Data collection, recording, and interpretation
* Problem solving

Sort It Out

Sorting helps us simplify a complex world. Even babies can sort. ("Who's Mommy, who's not?" "What's food? What's not?" "What won't hurt me? What might?") In kindergarten, children refine their classification skills to make information even more accessible.

Classification focuses attention on *similar attributes*. The finer the differentiation, the more challenging the sort, and the more valuable the information the system provides. (Imagine trying to find a favorite story in a library that sorts books into just nonfiction and fiction piles!)

As kindergartners group items and explain how items relate within the group, they develop powerful mathematical reasoning skills.

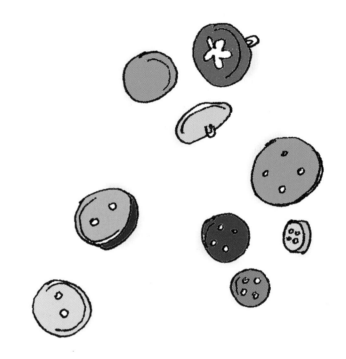

 ### Making Everyday Connections

Weave sorting experiences throughout the day, throughout the curriculum.

Cooking: Sort snacks such as trail mix, nuts, colored jelly beans, or cereal.

Social Studies: Sort community helpers (page 93) by those who need vehicles and those who don't.

Science: Sort animals by their movement, body covering, or number of legs.

Literacy: Sort words by their beginning sounds (page 24), rhyme families (page 23), or meaning.

Collection Fun!

MATERIALS: fun stuff to sort — stones, shells, keys (ask your local key shop for castoffs), buttons, nuts in shells, small plastic animals (available from educational supply or dollar stores), or small, safe hardware items

Children love to explore collections! Zip-locking bags of fun stuff instantly inspire my kindergartners to start grouping similar items together. As they group, guide children to reflect: *Why did you put those things together? Does this item belong in your group? Why or why not?*

Encourage kids to collect on their own, too. Treasuring stamps, sports cards, heart-shaped rocks, or crazy erasers develops a liking for *organization*. Kids start to take notice of how things are grouped together ("So *that's* why it's easy to find my cereal in the grocery store!") and how they are similar and different. ("Those trees lose their leaves, those don't.")

Cutout Collections. My kindergartners love digging through magazines with scissors in hand. So I capitalize on their zeal by having them think about categories

as they do so. Write words such as **food**, **actions**, and **vehicles** on separate sheets of paper. Have kids cut out and paste magazine pictures to match each category. Or, let them draw their own pictures and add word labels. I find this is also a great way to anchor vocabulary for words such as **tangerine**, **hiking**, or **vehicle** (see DEEPEN KIDS' UNDERSTANDING, page 14).

Secret Rule

PLAYERS: Any number!

Start by making a statement of what belongs, such as *In my house I have an orange.* Players ask questions to try to guess what the secret rule is by stating similar items. "How about a banana?" *No.* "How about a ball?" *Yes. Can you guess the secret rule?* "I know! Everything in your house is round!"

⟲DEEPEN kids' understanding

Kids clarify their reasoning and develop their language by thinking aloud: "I sorted by size" (or "color, critter, smooth stuff, things from nature," and so on). Challenging children to sort in a *different* way encourages flexible thinking: "Maybe I can sort these same tiles by shape instead of by color."

* ✳ *How did you decide on these groups?*
* ✳ *Does this thing go in your group? Why or why not?*
* ✳ *How else could you sort this stuff?*

Clues

PLAYERS: Any number!

The leader gives three clues to the identity of a secret item. *I'm thinking of something made of metal. It fits in your hand. It unlocks a door. What is it?* Kids ask investigative questions ("Can it start a car?") or guess until they get the answer ("A key!"). In my classroom, I enrich "share time" and add suspense by having kids hide their item in a bag and offer three clues. Classmates take turns guessing the item and practicing their inference skills.

There's a Pattern Here

Think about patterns, and suddenly the world is filled with *repeating sequences!* Patterns appear in nature (orange segments, ocean waves, cell division), in man-made materials (T-shirt stripes, floor tiles, suspension bridges), and, of course, in mathematics (the counting sequence, exponential growth, Fibonacci numbers).

Noticing Patterns

Pattern is one of the first forms of organized thinking children explore in kindergarten.

Observe. Point out patterns, and children will, too! Striped shirts, turtle shells, and fences are just a few. *What do you notice? Is it a pattern? How do you know?*

Explore. Let kids explore a pile of coins. Then model how to create a repeating linear pattern (penny, nickel, quarter, penny, nickel, quarter). *What other patterns can we make?*

Identify. It's quite easy for children to "read" their patterns: "red, red, green, red, red, green" . . . and so on. But it's challenging for them to identify just the repeating part ("It's a red-red-green pattern") or to state it in a generic way ("It's an AAB pattern"). *Can you read the pattern?*

See. It's a red, red, green pattern.

Once my kindergartners make this leap, they are able to flexibly transfer information to new situations, which is what learning is all about. Patterns start to pop up at our activity centers, "Now I can create an AAB pattern with beads on a necklace, raisins and peanuts, or by clapping and snapping!"

Pattern Play

Extend and strengthen pattern recognition with creative fun!

 ## Make a Patterned Bangle

MATERIALS: scissors, toilet-paper tube, colored paper, crayons or markers, glue

1. Cut 1.5" (3.5 cm) bangle bases from toilet-paper tubes (each tube will make three bases).

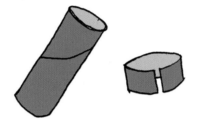

2. Cut 1.5" x 7" (3.5 x 17.5 cm) strips of colored paper. Create picture patterns (circle, heart, flower) on the strips using crayons or markers.

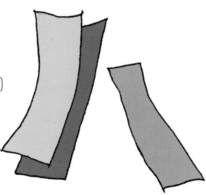

3. Glue a pattern strip onto the cardboard and wear your mathematical pattern creation!

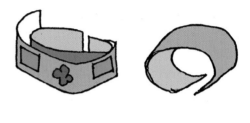

Challenge kids to think aloud. *Describe your pattern to me. How do you build a pattern?*

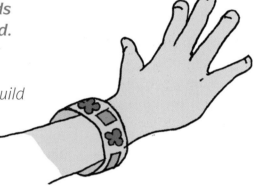

 Cap It! Model pattern building for children by beginning a pattern. Use colored milk-jug caps to begin a pattern: *red-red-blue-yellow, red-red-, ...* Make a game of players taking turns extending the pattern. *Which part repeats? What comes next?*

DEEPEN kids' understanding

Get Physical! Assign actions to words such as **clap, snap, cross** (arms crossed on chest), **tug** (tug ears), or **slap** (slap thighs). Call out a pattern — this works well if you're waiting in line — or start a pattern and have kids join in. Let children take turns creating their own action patterns for others to follow.

Investigate 2-D Designs

MATERIALS: grid paper, crayons or markers
Color in squares on 1" (2.5 cm) grid paper to create two-dimensional designs. These might be checkerboard, stripes, or concentric masterpieces. Or, build 2-D designs with colored math tiles or 1" (2.5 cm) colorful cardstock squares.

Jamie's Masterpiece

Making Everyday Connections

Weave pattern experiences into the day and throughout the curriculum.

Cooking: Explore patterns in layer cakes, lasagna, and fruit and veggie snack arrangements.

Music: Investigate rhythmic patterns and musical refrains such as "The Farmer in the Dell."

Science: Look for patterns in the change of seasons, day to night, and life cycles.

Literacy: Find patterns in word families (**cat, bat, rat,** and so on) and stories (*The Three Bears*; *Is Your Mama a Llama?* by Deborah Guarino; *Brown Bear, Brown Bear, What Do You See?* by Bill Martin Jr.).

What's a Number?

Children come to school with some sense of number. A toddler learns from six raisins. One by one she pops them into her mouth and watches as her precious pile grows smaller. Mom gives her three more. Is this as many as what she had?

Kindergartners expand their understanding through concrete experiences that lay the foundation for more abstract work to come. The number 9 is not just a balloon shape on a flash card. It's an idea to use flexibly — an amount less than 12, a place in the number sequence, a 3-by-3 array, 4 + 5, and more. Kids construct this understanding by using manipulatives, games, and life experiences to count, group, and play with numbers.

$6 + 3 = 9$

$13 - 4 = 9$

Count!

Count kids, coins, candy, time ... anything, anytime! Chant to practice the *rote order* of the number names. Count "stuff" to build the concept of *one-to-one correspondence* and *quantity*.

Practice the counting sequence

Count to the Beat! Clap, stretch arms, stomp feet, jump. Let kids come up with more motions to count to a steady beat.

... 17 ... 18 ... 19 ... 20

Echo. You say *one* (or *1, 2, 3*). Kids say "two" (or "4, 5, 6"). Continue counting.

Repair It! If counting sounds like this: " ... 11, 12, 14, 15," focus on just the part that needs repair. I find my kindergartners get it right when they repeat the tricky part again and again in sing-song way, **11**, *12*, **13**, *14*, **15** ...,

Making Everyday Connections

Share traditional counting songs and rhymes. Can't remember the words? Search these titles on the Internet: "1, 2, Buckle My Shoe"; "Ten Little Monkeys"; "Over in the Meadow"; "100 Bottles of Coke on the Wall"; "Five Little Ducks"; "Five Little Speckled Frogs"; "One Potato, Two Potato."

Explore one-to-one correspondence and quantity

 **Counting Mats**

MATERIALS: crayons, paper plates, card stock, counters (beans, shells, fish crackers)

1. You or the child draws a picture on a plate to match the counters — a beach scene if kids are counting a collection of shells; a watermelon slice for counting black beans; a fishbowl for counting fish crackers.

2. Write numbers 1 through 20 on 2" (5 cm) squares of card stock. Kids set any number card on a plate, then count out a matching amount of counters.

3. Remove everything from the plate. Pick a new number and count again!

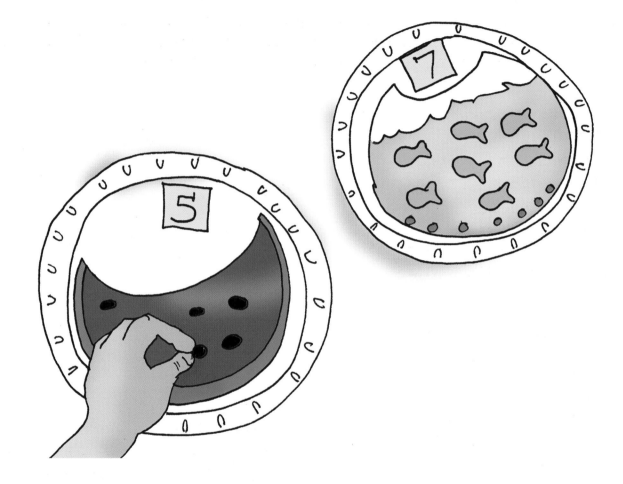

Touch and Count. *How many peanuts in the pile?* Solving a problem makes counting meaningful, and using kid-friendly counters makes it fun! Remind children to *touch,* *say the number name,* and *move each item* to a new pile for accurate counting.

Compare!

I think it's interesting that my kindergartners who always like to be the winner seem to know the words *more* and *most. Less, least, and equal* are often new concepts. Learning these math concepts through the social interaction of a game builds understanding.

 ## More!

PLAYERS: 2

MATERIALS: 1 or 2 decks of playing cards

This is a variation on the classic card game War. To play, divide the deck (or two decks) between two players. Keep card piles face down. Players flip over the top card and read the numbers aloud. The player with the larger number shouts "More!" and takes both cards. If the numbers are equal, lay out three more cards and flip the next cards.

Kids can also play LESS with the smaller number winning each round. *Who has the most cards after all are flipped?*

Eggs and Nests

PLAYERS: 2

MATERIALS: 6 marbles, 6 milk-jug caps, die, paper, pencil

One player has six marbles (eggs); the other has six milk-jug caps (nests). On her turn, the player rolls a die to determine how many eggs or nests to put in the center. Place one egg inside each nest for easy comparison. *Is there an extra egg or an empty nest?* Count who has the greater number after each round, and keep track of the winner of each round with tally marks. Ten tallies wins!

Variation: The lower number wins the round.

Reading and Writing Numbers

Kindergartners are expected to learn to write and identify numerals from 0 to 30, typically. (Check your state standards to see what numbers kindergartners in your area must master.) Reading and writing numbers can be learned using many of the same multisensory practices kids use for learning letters (see MAKING SENSE OF THE ALPHABET, page 20).

 ## Make a Number-Search Crown

MATERIALS: scissors, old newspapers or magazines, glue, construction paper, stapler

Kids cut numbers from advertisements and glue them down in order on a long strip of paper. *How far can you go?* Make the strip into a crown by stapling it to fit around the child's head.

Concentration. Make your own deck of 12 to 20 index cards, with two cards for each number the child is learning. Place the cards face down. Kids flip over two at a time and call out the numbers. If the numbers match, the player keeps the pair.

Road Bingo.
Pick numbers between 1 and 30 to write on a 5-by-5 grid. Place on a clipboard. Players mark off the numbers they see on the go: speed-limit signs, advertising, license plates. First one across, down, or diagonal yells "Bingo!"

Reasonable guesses, or "guesstimates," are useful and show a high level of number sense: *About how many pounds of peaches should we buy? How long will it take to get to the park? Can you jump farther than a meter?* Encourage kids to blend number sense with experience to come up with a thoughtful estimate, not the exact number or a wild guess.

Here's what a pile of 10 gummy worms looks like. So, how many do you think we'll need to file this jar? "15?" *Let's count and see.*

Trace around your hand or foot. Guess how many pennies will fill the space. "20!" *Fill the area with pennies. Then count and see if you were close!*

It's All Fun and Games ... and Math!

Work number sense into everyday play.

Card games: Young children love to play Go Fish. What else can you do with a deck of cards? Sort by color, suit, or number; create four sequenced sets of ace through 10 (or king); pick two cards and find their sum; play Concentration with two sets of ace through king; play Old Maid with two sets of ace through king and a joker.

Board games: Bingo, Chutes and Ladders, Hi Ho! Cherry-O, Cootie, Uno, Connect Four, Trouble, and any board games where kids count each move.

Dice and domino games.

Number Combos

Kindergartners discover that numbers are made up of smaller numbers. Unique pairs, such as 0 and 5, 1 and 4, and 2 and 3, always make up the number 5, for instance. Exploring this concept in several ways builds a strong foundation for *addition* and *subtraction*.

 Story Strips

Make your own story strips to explore addition and subtraction!

MATERIALS: scissors, business-size envelope, markers or crayons, letter-size white paper

Make the story strip

1. Cut a sealed envelope in half and at one end to make a sleeve. Print the target number (4) on the sleeve.

2. Cut sheets of paper in thirds the long way to create paper strips that fit through the sleeve. Draw a guideline about 2 1/2" (6 cm) from one end of a strip.

3. Have kids draw groups of ladybugs (or balloons, hearts, dogs, and so on) on either side of the guideline to total the target number (4).

Explore number combinations

Slip the strip through the sleeve to expose one group and hide the other. Ask: *There are four ladybug friends. One came out to play. How many are hiding?* Let kids find out by pulling the strip to reveal the answer. Introduce subtraction by showing both groups on the story strip. Then say: *There were four ladybugs. Two flew away.* (Hide in sleeve.) *How many are left?* (Count the exposed group.)

Extend the learning

Make more story strips for the number 4. Then explore other numbers. *How did you predict how many balloons* (or *ladybugs, hearts,* etc.) *were hiding?*

Black Beans, White Beans

MATERIALS: permanent marker, 10 dried white flat beans (such as lima beans), paper

Use the marker to color one side of the 10 beans. Give kids a target number, such as 5, to explore:

Toss. *Toss five beans. Which color lands up?*

Group. *Group the beans by color.*

Count. *Count the beans in each group.*

Say. *Three black beans and two white beans make five beans altogether!*

Record. Make a sketch of black and white (outlined) beans, labeled with numbers to record each toss. Show kids how to write an equation as another way to record their bean toss.

Keep tossing until all combinations are discovered several times. Explore other target numbers through 10.

T-Time

MATERIALS: index card, pennies

Draw a "T" on a 3" x 5" (7.5 cm x 12.5 cm) index card. Set a target number of pennies, say 6, on top to explore. Let kids:

Group. *Set pennies on either side of the line.*

Count. *How many are on each side?*

Record. Write down the number combinations. 2 + 4, 3 + 3 . . .

Help kids notice that the total always stays the same. *Look how many pairs make the number 6!*

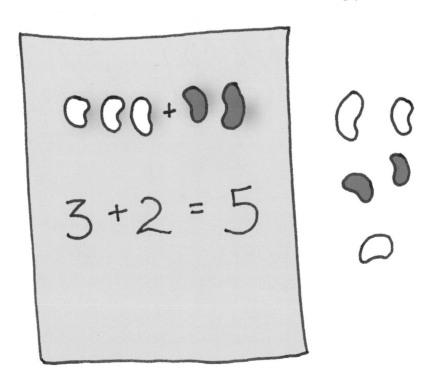

Making Everyday Connections

Our classroom learning centers give my kindergartners an authentic way to practice number combinations. *There can be five kids in the art center. There are only two there now. How many more may paint?*
At home, there are many possibilities:

There are two forks on the table. How many more do we need for our family?

We have four apples and two bananas. How many fruits do we have?

Our mini-van has seven sets of seat belts. We are using four. How many more kids could we invite on this trip?

⟲DEEPEN kids' understanding

Build number sense as children work with combinations by asking key questions:

✳ *What was the total every time?* (the target number)

✳ *How many combinations could you make? Are there more?*

✳ *Does the number 5 have more pairs than the number 4?*

Shape Up!

Exploring shape builds visual thinking. It gives kids another way to make sense of their world. From home fix-it projects to engineering bridges, geometry is an essential real-life skill. In kindergarten, children focus on *identifying* and *comparing* basic two-dimensional shapes (triangle, square, rectangle, circle) and are introduced to 3-D shapes (sphere, cone, cube).

Exploring Triangle-ness

What makes a triangle a triangle? Once kids discover a triangle's characteristics, they can find them, compare them, and create their own!

Define the shape

Set out several triangles. *How are they alike? What do you notice? Let's count the sides and corners.* Together, create a kid-friendly definition: *So, a triangle is a flat shape with only three sides and three corners.*

Contrast

Set out several shapes. *Can you sort the triangles from the rest?*

Create!

👤 **Feely Shapes.** Make triangles on paper from toothpicks, straw segments, yarn, or pipe cleaners.

👤 **Make a Puzzle**

MATERIALS: paper, scissors

Fold and trim a sheet of 8¹/₂" x 11" paper (21 cm x 27.5 cm) to make a large triangle. Have kids fold the paper triangle two or three times, then open it up and cut along the fold lines. *What shapes did you discover? Can you put your triangle back together?*

👤 **Triangle Art**

MATERIALS: scissors, construction paper, glue, markers or crayons

Cut out all sorts of triangles from colored paper. Have kids lay them on a sheet of larger paper, trying different designs. *Do your triangles remind you of something familiar?* Glue down the triangles and use crayons or markers to add details to the pictures.

Extend the learning

Explore other shapes this way. Then have kids compare numbers of sides and corners on all the shapes they have studied and sort shapes into same-shape piles.

⦿DEEPEN *kids' understanding*

Not all shapes are flat. Discover how shapes are also three-dimensional!

Compare a circle (a quarter or a CD) to a sphere (ball) or cylinder (jar); a square to a cube; a triangle to a pyramid or cone. *How are they alike? Different?*

About Face. Help kids see how flat shapes can be found on the faces of 3-D shapes. *How many rectangles can you find on this cereal box?*

Something New. Cut an ice cream carton along the seams, *Look, there's a circle and a big rectangle.* Cut along the spiral seam of a toilet-paper tube. *It's just a rolled up trapezoid!*

Making Everyday Connections

Go on a Shape Hunt!

Encourage kids to search out shapes to see their world in a new way. Draw a shape, such as a triangle, at the top of a sheet of paper attached to a clipboard. Send kids out to look for triangles in the classroom, home, or yard. *Sketch and label what you find!* Repeat with other shapes.

Measure It!

Measurement activities clearly link math skills with real-life experiences. "Who's taller?" "Is it lunchtime?" "How much ice cream is left?" In kindergarten, children compare *length*, *weight*, and *capacity of objects*; develop a sense of *time*; and experiment with *tools and units for measurement*.

Measure Me

MATERIALS: yarn, scissors, picture or index card and marker, tape

Have kids work together or with a mentor to measure themselves. One child lays down and her friend cuts a length of yarn to match her height. Tape a picture or name label to one end of the yarn, and tape the other tip to the wall. A classroom of kids can compare and sequence their height strands.

Measure More

Use yarn to measure the height of a bookcase, the perimeter of a tree trunk, a (friendly!) dog from nose to tail tip. Have kids draw a sketch to show how they made the measurement. Tape each sketch to the appropriate yarn measure. Compare yarn lengths.

Note: Remind kids to always align the object and the measuring tool on a baseline!

Fill 'er Up! Explore volume by filling cup measures, quart-sized plastic containers, and clean half-gallon and gallon milk jugs. Add to a water table, sand center, or bathtub.

 Weight for Me. Balance scales let kids compare the weight of blocks, toys, fruit, and other small objects. Encourage kids to sketch what they observe, then write a conclusion: "The bear weighs more than the frog because that end drops lower."

No tape measure needed!

The width of hand has been used to measure a horse, and a stride was once used to measure land. Get into the act by letting kids try their own nonstandard units of measurement to appreciate the origins of measurement! Have kids draw a sketch to show how many units were used.

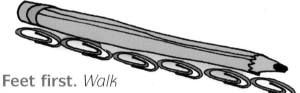

Feet first. *Walk heel to toe to measure the length of a room. Count your steps.*

Clips. *Lay clips end to end to measure a pencil, fork, or spine of a book. Count how many you used.*

Crayons. *Lay new crayons end to end to measure the edge of a desk or length of your friend's arm. How many did you need?*

WEIghTY Words

I integrate literacy with my math centers by posting key words for recording discoveries. These word cards are prominent at the weight center: **weighs, more than, less than, the same as, because, lower, higher, level**

Telling Time

Kindergartners learn to tell time to the hour. Point out activities that happen on the hour throughout the day. *Look, it's 7:00 in the morning; time to get up. It's 12:00, so that means it's lunchtime!*

Time for lunch!

DEEPEN kids' understanding

Have children organize their discoveries by making mini record-books (see page 85), showing one labeled picture on each page. Suggest these measurement topics:

* Things that are longer than a ruler.
* Activities that take less than one minute (use an egg timer).
* Objects that are heavier than an apple.
* What I do at different times of day.

Making Everyday Connections

Science: Measure the length of kids' shadows throughout the day.

Physical Education: Measure and compare the distance kids can jump.

Cooking: Let kids do the measuring of ingredients!

Geography: Watch the odometer on the car or use a map to measure distances from home to school, stores, the library, or a park.

Take a Survey

My kindergartners' favorite topic for discovery is each other! Add to that hot areas of interest such as favorite ice cream flavors, colors, or pets, and I can't keep them from engaging in high-level math! Kids design a survey, collect data, record the results, and then come to a conclusion — all by themselves! Just hand a child a clipboard, pencil, and survey sheet and let the fun begin.

 Survey It

MATERIALS: paper, markers

Make the survey sheet
Create simple survey sheets. Start with a two-column yes/no style.

Design the investigation
Help children write their question on the survey form. "Have you ever flown on an airplane?" Or: "What are your favorite snacks?"

While it's easier to give children questions to survey, having them generate their own is far more meaningful. It lets them know their curiosity and interests are valued. I find I must teach children how to formulate a question. First, we brainstorm all the ways we can be different from or similar to one another (hair color and style, number of people in our families, number of letters in our names, if we have pets, our experiences, our preferences ...). Then I model how to set these up as a question. *Can you make a paper airplane? Which is your favorite park?* Soon, they are wondering all sorts of fascinating things to ask about each other!

Take the survey

1. **Gather data.** Circulate your survey among friends, classmates, and family members to gather responses. Kids can gather data by making tally marks, coloring in cells for each response, having respondents write their name in the cell. Remind children to record data from the baseline upward so that the data appears as an accurate graph.

Favorite Snacks

apple   pizza   trail mix   ice cream

2. **Interpret the data.** Count yes and no responses. "Six kids have flown on an airplane. four kids have not."

3. **Draw conclusions!** "I know that the number 6 is more than 4. So, more kids in my class (people in my family) have flown on an airplane than not."

Survey Speak

Model and encourage kids to use words that promote data analysis: **most, least, more than, less than, equal**

⊙DEEPEN kids' understanding

Formulating questions is challenging. Mentors model by starting kids out with pre-structured surveys. Then, encourage kids to generate questions of interest to them. Kids can pose questions across all aspects of kid life.

Yes/No questions

Have your ever ... lost a tooth, broken a bone, gone camping?

Can you ... tie your shoes, make a peanut butter sandwich, ride a two-wheeler?

Multiple-response questions

Pick a favorite ... snack (pizza, ice cream, or strawberries), pet (dog, cat, fish), season (spring, summer, fall, winter).

Just the facts

Kids can also track factual information, not based on opinions:

How many heads (or tails) come up after 10 tosses of a coin?

How many kids ... have five, less than five, or more than five letters in their name? ... are wearing pants, shorts, or skirts today?

How many of a color in a handful of ... M&M's, Froot Loops cereal, Skittles?

So, more kids wear shorts on a hot day!

I Figured It Out!

Good questions coach kids in figuring out ways to find answers independently: *What are you trying to find out? What do you know? How can you use objects or a sketch to model the problem? How did you think that through?*

Opportunities that engage kids in applying their skills and understanding to solve multifaceted, realistic problems inspire mathematical thinking beyond the kindergarten classroom. Skills are learned not as ends in themselves. The ultimate goal is for kids to gain a valuable tool for solving real-life problems.

Model Step-by-Step Problem Solving

1. Listen. *Two yellow ducks are in the pond. Three brown ducks came. How many ducks are in the pond now?*

2. Think. *What do you need to find out? What do you already know that will help you find the answer?*

3. Make a sketch or model. Draw a picture of the story or use objects to make a model.

4. Label. Add number labels to each group.

5. Solve. *How can you figure out how many ducks there are altogether? We can count through both groups! One, two, three, four, five.*

6. State the equation. Write a number sentence (equation) that represents the story. **2 + 3 = 5.**

7. Challenge. Write or retell the story with words. *How many ways can you tell a number story?* With pictures, objects, numbers, and words!

DEEPEN *kids' understanding*

Challenge children's problem-solving skills with multifaceted questions:

Two clowns each hold two balloons. How many balloons in all?

How many hands in our family?

Three dogs play in the park. How many paws are there?

Making Everyday Connections

I know that flexible thinking and problem solving are essential skills for my students. So, to figure out our daily attendance, sometimes we simply count children. On other days, we figure out how many are absent, then count backward on a number line from the number of enrolled. Seize opportunities to problem-solve throughout the day!

Each kid at the birthday party will get three balloons. How many should we buy?

How many Valentines should we buy for your classmates, teacher, and class helpers?

We need four eggs to make a cake. We have two. How many more must we buy?

Science

Exploring how the world works

Young children are natural scientists: They're on a relentless quest to understand how the world works. Kindergartners build understanding through investigation, just as grown-up scientists do. They *ask questions* ("How come I can't fly?"), *observe* carefully ("Look at this sparkly rock!"), *gather and analyze information* ("That bug curls into a ball when I pick it up"), and *test predictions and explanations* ("I bet this snowball will make a puddle if I bring it inside"). An effective kindergarten science program nurtures a young child's natural drive to seek answers by focusing on these inquiry skills.

Children come to see science as a powerful learning tool when it supports what they love to do — make discoveries about their world!

It's Standard!
Kindergartners develop *investigation skills* (observe, describe, compare, analyze, predict, communicate) while learning science content in:

* Physical Science
* Earth Science
* Life Science

Dripping with Physical Science

Splash in water and feel it slosh on your skin. Pour water from bottles into jars and watch it take on any shape. Notice the elegant form of a water droplet. Observe a puddle on a sunny day and see how it vanishes!

Physical science in kindergarten explores the *properties of materials*. Because water is so dynamic (and so much fun to explore!), it is a rich medium through which to learn about physical science and apply budding inquiry skills.

⚓ Water Lab!

There's an instant science lab in a drop of water. This activity takes kids' thinking from observing to describing to comparing to predicting. Then, after conducting water investigations, kindergartners communicate their understanding through technology by becoming designers! Along the way, they discover *surface tension*, the amazing force that lets water act as if it has a skin, causing it to form a fascinating dome shape.

MATERIALS

* Swatches and small items for discovery, such as pieces of different kinds of cloth (terry, denim, knit), waxed paper, magazine pages, cardboard, newspaper, paper towel, napkin, tissue paper, foil, plastic wrap, leaves, cotton ball, sponge; enough for two different observation days

* Droppers (see TOOLS OF THE TRADE, page 72)
* Cup of water
* Index cards
* Markers or crayons
* Hand lens (see TOOLS OF THE TRADE, page 72)
* Paper (for drawing)

Explore and observe

Let children use droppers or their fingers to drip water on each swatch or small item. View at eye level. *What do you notice? Yes, sometimes the water soaks into the material. We say the water is "absorbed." Sometimes the water forms a hump or dome shape on the material. We say the water is "repelled."*

absorb

sponge

newspaper

cotton

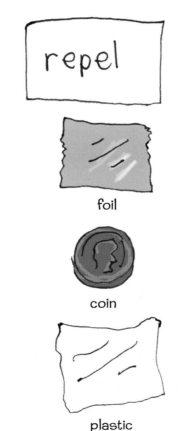

repel

foil

coin

plastic

Compare and conclude

Write the words **Absorb** and **Repel** on two index cards with a marker or crayon. *Sort the materials beneath Absorb and Repel word cards, based on your discoveries. Then, use a hand lens to examine the materials more closely.*

How are the materials the same within each group? What do you notice about those that repelled the water? Yes, they are very smooth. The materials that absorbed the water had many tiny nooks among the fibers. The water must have filled those tiny crannies.

Predict

Offer children a different collection of swatches and small items. Based on their water-behavior discoveries, have them sort the items into groups: those they predict will *absorb* water and those they predict will *repel* a drop of water. Have kids use a hand lens to help with their predictions. *How are you deciding on your predictions?*

Test and see!

Let children test their predictions by placing a drop on each material. *Did you make reasonable guesses?*

Problem-solve

Invite kids to be designers. *You are a water expert. What materials would you use to make the best raincoat? Draw a picture of gear to keep you dry (repel water). Then design and draw a gizmo to sop up spills (absorb water). Label the materials you use in each picture.*

Tools of the Trade

Scientists use tools to enhance their understanding; so can young children!

Dropper. Squeeze, dunk, release, lift, squeeze. After playing with a plastic meat-baster or dropper in a tub of water, kids become pro! No dropper? Fold a drinking straw a third of the way down for an instant dropper.

FOLD STRAW

Hand lens. The key to great viewing is to put the viewer near the specimen, not your eye! Move slightly to bring the specimen into focus.

DEEPEN kids' understanding

I often ask my kindergartners to communicate their science discoveries by recording them. They might record (write or draw) any step of the inquiry process: *prediction, observation, conclusion, what they wonder.* We use no work sheets. By working on blank paper, they construct understanding in their own ways. Records range from scribbles to fancy diagrams. They might use arrows to show ideas or labels to describe features, just like the diagrams we look at in read-aloud informational text. I find the recording step builds accountability into their explorations. It helps them see science as a disciplined way of thinking that they are capable of doing, too.

DROp Power

Tension at the surface of a liquid creates the effect of a skin.
Offer children ways to experience this phenomenon in new contexts.

⚓ Take the Penny Challenge!

Pennies in a cup. Set a glass on a plate and fill it almost to the brim with water. *How many pennies do you predict we can add to the glass without the water spilling over? View the glass rim at eye level. What do you notice? What does the water do?*

Drops on a penny. Set a penny on a plate. *How many drops of water do you predict the penny can hold?* Use a medicine dropper and start dripping. *What shape is the water?*

⚓ Stretchy Water

Soap reduces surface tension and allows water to stretch into a thin film that surrounds a puff of air. Bubbles always take the shape with the least possible surface area. *What shape is every bubble no matter which blower you use?* "A sphere!"

Bubble Brew

MATERIALS

* ❋ 1/2 cup (125 ml) liquid dishwashing detergent (Joy or Dawn work well)
* ❋ 4 cups (1 L) water
* ❋ 3 to 4 tablespoons (45 to 60 ml) corn syrup

Gently mix ingredients in a plastic storage bottle.

Kids can use almost anything to blow bubbles: their hands; pipe cleaners formed into a circle, heart, square, or any shape at one end; plastic six-pack beverage holders; cans with both ends open; plastic coat hangers; soda straws; and funnels.

Mystery Bubbles: Fill a soda bottle with Bubble Brew. Cover the opening with your hand as you turn the bottle upside down. Slowly empty the brew into a bowl. Have kids observe the results. *Is the bottle empty? What do you notice inside? Why do you think these bubbles have weird shapes? The bubbles in the bottle are packed into a tight space. So each bubble changes shape to make room for the rest.*

Wonderful Water

There is so much more to wonder about water!

 ## Changing Shapes

Guide kindergartners to discover key characteristics of water. Offer kids a variety of plastic containers in the tub or at a water table. *What happens when you pour water? Which way does it always flow? How can you change water's shape?*

 ## Float or Sink?

MATERIALS: clear container of water, a variety of objects (key, rock, cork, spoon, Ping-Pong ball, birthday candle), paper, markers

What do objects do in water? Invite kids to make predictions. *Which objects will sink? Which will float? Draw a sketch of your prediction. How will you know if your guesses are right? Yes, test and see! Drop the items in a clear container of water. Now draw a sketch of what you actually observed.*

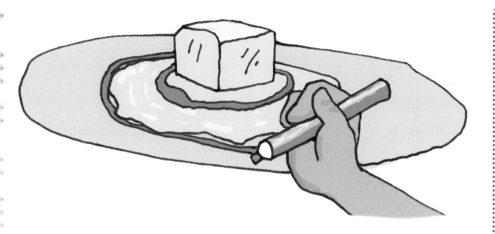

 Absorbent Art

Drip food coloring or watercolors onto a coffee filter. *What happens to the drops?*

Art Resist

Draw a picture on art paper by pressing hard with crayons. Paint a watercolor wash over the picture. *Why doesn't your picture disappear?*

It's Just a Phase! Help kindergartners discover that solid ice melts into liquid water and eventually evaporates into an invisible vapor.

Observe an ice cube melting throughout the day. Set it on a coated paper plate and use a crayon to periodically outline the puddle. *How does the puddle change? What happens overnight?* For dramatic results, have kids observe as you fry ice cubes in a pan!

 **Blow It!**

Drip watercolors onto white paper. Blow the drops with a straw to make flowing patterns.

Earth Science Rocks!

What can be more amazing than holding a piece of our planet, maybe a million years old, in the palm of your hand? By collecting rocks, kindergartners practice comparing and describing skills. They discover that *rock* is a hard, nonliving substance that comes from the earth and is formed in different ways; *sand* is a gritty, nonliving substance that comes from broken rock; and *soil* is made of sand and bits of dead plants and animals. Help kids discover the wonderful world beneath their feet!

⚓ Start a Rock Collection

Collecting rocks is a universal kid-pursuit. Add inquiry skills, and you've got the perfect lesson for a budding geologist!

When a child comes up with about 20 rock finds, encourage her to sort the specimens by any of the following ways:

Size. Group by size. *Can you sequence from smallest to largest rock?*

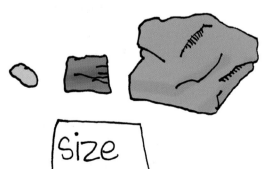

Shape. Flat, oval . . . *Can you find a round rock?*

Appearance. Speckles, layers, colors . . . *Which are darkest? Lightest?*

 ROCK OUT!

What else can you do with your rock collection? Plenty!

Pebble Pictures. Use a 9" x 12" (22.5 x 30 cm) piece of black felt as a backdrop for a pebble design. Kids can lay pebbles out in fascinating shapes, lines, and patterns. A perfect rainy-day toy!

Rock and Roll. Kids can make rock sounds by tapping different rocks together. *Do different rocks make different sounds?* Roll pebbles around on a metal pie plate, a plastic lid, or a towel. *Why do the pebble sounds change?*

Pet Rock. *Does the shape of your rock remind you of an animal?* Children can use acrylic or tempera paint and a small brush to make the rock look like a critter.

Feel. Jagged, smooth, bumpy . . . *Close your eyes. Touch the rocks. Now, sort!*

Hardness. Put rocks to the test. *Which rocks can be rubbed with fingers? Scratched with a plastic spoon? Scratched with a penny? Which rocks don't scratch easily? So, which must be the softest rocks? Which are the hardest? What makes you think so?*

Streak-ability. Invite children to use rocks to make streaks on pavement, then try sorting rocks by the color of the streaks. *Rocks are made of different ingredients called "minerals." Geologists use streak tests to identify these minerals.*

My Way. Invite children to develop their own classification scheme. *Explain your sort.*

What's Cooking? Rocks!

Cooking makes wonderful rock models. Why? The earth moves, mixes, presses, and heats ingredients called minerals into rocks. Model the origins of the three classes of rocks — *metamorphic, igneous,* and *sedimentary* — right in the kitchen or classroom for hands-on earth science experiences!

A Cookie Model?

A cookie is not a rock, of course. But in some ways a cookie is *like* a rock. Models give children (and grown-up scientists) a way to conceptualize science. They help build understanding by using familiar materials at a scale kids can manipulate. Using models, complicated processes (such as how rock is formed from the earth's magma) can be made simple.

Like all young children, my kindergartners are literal thinkers. I've heard misunderstandings such as "We made rocks in the oven!" Now, I never walk away from an experience like this without clarifying our learning, *Rocks are not really cooked in an oven, but in the earth's core, where it's even hotter!*

Igneous Meltdown

Magma is rock that melts from heat and pressure deep within the earth. Sometimes magma comes out on the earth's surface through a volcano as *lava*. As it cools and hardens, it turns into igneous rock.

Explore how chocolate "lava" hardens as it cools into "igneous candy"!

MATERIALS: oven-proof nonmetal bowl, different flavors of candy chips, spoon, plate or small dish, ice cream (optional)

1. Chocolate, white chocolate, peanut butter, and butterscotch chips are like the different kinds of minerals that make up rocks. Microwave a cup of chips in a microwave-safe bowl for two minutes on medium. Stir well. Microwave at 30-second intervals until the chips melt into "magma."

2. Pour the liquid rock onto a plate. *This is like lava flowing on the earth's surface.*

3. Let the lava harden and cool. Break it up into igneous rock candy. For more fun, pour the lava over a volcano-shaped ice cream mound!

Flow on the Go!

Hawaii was created millions of years ago from volcanoes deep on the ocean floor. The island continues to grow as lava flows from Kilauea (kee-law-WAY-ah) — the world's most active crater, on the slope of Mauna Loa. Kids can view a live cam of the action at the website for Hawaii Volcanoes National Park, **www.nps.gov/havo**.

⚓ Sedimentary Sandwich

Pile up mud, sand, and dead plants and animals.
Smash these layers together over hundreds of thousands of
years. What do you have? *Sedimentary rock!*

MATERIALS: plate; peanut butter, honey, or cream cheese; brown sugar; sunflower seeds; banana slices or raisins; bread slices or graham crackers

1. Explain: *Think of the plate as a river bottom, where sedimentary rock is often formed. Creatively layer "mud" (peanut butter, honey, or cream cheese), "sand" (brown sugar), "bones" (sunflower seeds), and "plants" (thin banana slices or raisins) between bread slices or graham crackers.*

2. *Press down lightly on your stacks. Each press represents the hundreds of thousands of years each layer presses down on the next. Which layers do you think are the oldest . . . the newest? What makes you think so?*

Hmmm ... I wonder

Although it's difficult to classify random rock samples, you can purchase specimens with obvious features: glassy, igneous obsidian; layered, sedimentary sandstone; swirled, metamorphic migmatite. You don't need to be a geologist to observe the details and speculate how a rock was formed. Getting it right is not the goal. Most important is to nurture a mindset of wonder.

Metamorphic Munchies

Think "rock," and change is not likely a concept that comes to mind. Yet rocks *do* change dramatically. Sure, it takes hundreds of thousands of years, but all three kinds of rock can be morphed through heat and compression to make new, dense metamorphic rock.

Explain as you begin: *Think of each ingredient as a "mineral" that will become part of a metamorphic cookie.*

Materials

- Mixing bowls, mixing spoons, measuring cups, beater, baking sheets
- 1 cup (250 ml) butter or margarine
- 1 cup (250 ml) brown sugar
- 1/2 cup (125 ml) white sugar
- 1 egg
- 1 cup (250 ml) flour
- 2 tsp (10 ml) baking soda
- 2 cups (500 ml) quick-cooking oats
- 1 1/2 cups (375 ml) of any combination of chocolate, butterscotch, or peanut butter chips, chopped nuts, or raisins

1. In a large bowl, cream the butter and sugars. Beat in the egg.
2. In a separate bowl, mix flour and baking soda. Add to the creamed mixture.
3. Stir in the oats. Stir in the chips, nuts, and raisins.
4. Use "pressure" to form 1/2-inch balls. Place on lightly greased baking sheets.

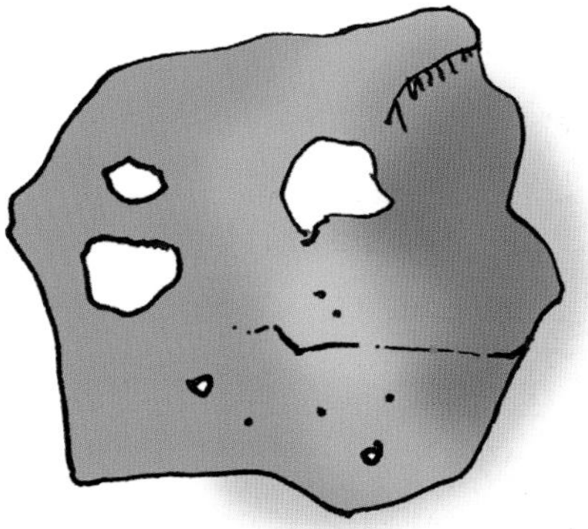

Knobby Gray Marble

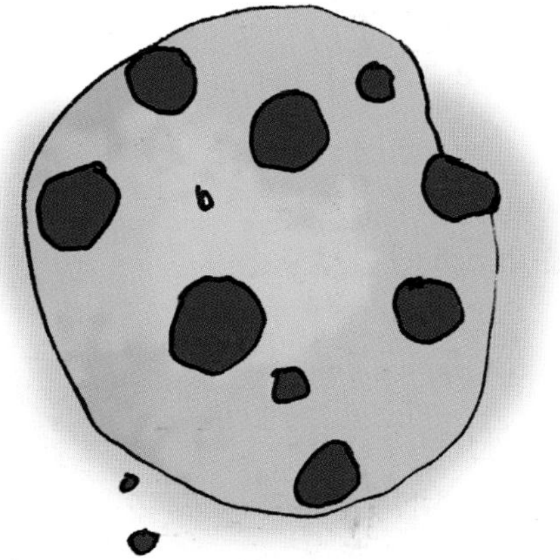

Metamorphic Munchie

5. Use "heat" to bake in a 350°F (180°C) oven for 10 to 12 minutes. Let cool.
6. Break a cookie apart. *Which "minerals" can you still see?* (Raisins, chips, nuts.) *Which have morphed into something new?* (Flour, sugar, oatmeal, egg, butter.) Eat the whole thing, and enjoy!

DEEPEN kids' understanding

Where's the Rock?

It's in sand. Rain and wind break rocks down into tiny pieces. Have children break a cookie down into tiny crumbs to understand that sand is simply particles of rock.

It's in soil. Half fill a plastic jar with soil. Add water to almost fill the jar. Seal the lid and shake. Now wait and observe how the soil settles. *What's at the bottom?* (Sand and bits of rock.) *What's at the top?* (Bits of dead plants and animal bones.) *Soil is made up of sand, rocks, and bits of dead plants and animals.*

So, how are soil, sand, and rock the same? They all come from the earth. They all have rock in them.

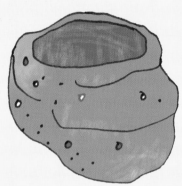 Art is a wonderful media for appreciating earth materials.

Soil Painting. Mix different colors of soil with water in small tubs. Have children brush these natural paints onto paper.

Sand Sculpture. Heat 2 cups (500 ml) sand, 1 cup (250 ml) cornstarch, and 1 cup (250 ml) water in an old pot. Stir as the mixture thickens. When cool, children can make a lasting sand castle or shape.

Rock Art. Clean a smooth rock. Provide tempera or acrylic paints. Encourage children to paint the rock in a way inspired by its shape.

Seeds of Life Science

A seed is a tiny treasure. Add water, and a new plant comes to life! Kindergartners are drawn to anything that's a "baby": infants, puppies, and baby plants (sprouts). Germinating seeds is a fun, fascinating way for children to safely experience life science up close.

Through seed study, kindergartners observe and record the growth of living things. They learn that living things have special structures to help them survive.

⚓ Open the Package!

A seed is a neat package. The baby plant (embryo) is packed with its food and surrounded by a protective cover (the seed coat).

Soak a handful of large bean seeds overnight until soft. Peel off the coat and split the beans in half. *Can you find the embryo? Just look at all that food for the new plant! Draw and label what you see. How does each part help the new plant survive?*

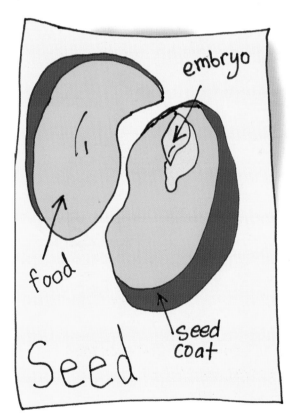

Make a See-Through Garden

MATERIALS: paper towels, glass jar, large seeds (beans, peas, corn) soaked overnight, water, SEED JOURNAL (page 85)

1. Fold a paper towel and roll it to fit up against the inside walls of a jar. Crumple a second paper towel and stuff it in the center.

2. Slip soaked seeds between the glass and the rolled towel. Add about an inch of water to the jar. *What do you think will happen to the seeds? What makes you think so?*

3. Set the jar in a sunny spot. Watch what happens over the next few days or weeks, and have kids track their observations in a SEED JOURNAL (see page 85). *Which way is the root growing? How about the stem and leaves? Why? Where do you think the sprout is getting its food?* Talk with children about when and why sprouts need to be planted in soil.

Scientific Salad

Discuss plant parts as you enjoy a salad. *What is the name of this plant? What part of the plant do you think it is?*

Leaves: lettuce, spinach

Flowers: broccoli, cauliflower, artichoke

Stems: celery, asparagus, broccoli

Roots: carrot, radish, beet

Fruit (flesh covering a seed): bell pepper, cucumber, tomato

Seeds: sesame, corn, sunflower, poppy

Day 12

Keep a Seed Journal

MATERIALS: scissors, paper, binder ring, markers and crayons

Young botanists can keep track of seed growth by drawing and labeling what they see. Cut paper into large seed shapes for the journal covers and pages. Fasten together with a binder ring. Help kids date their entries and write descriptions. Every change calls for a new page.

Indoor Seed Search. Some seeds are nutritious for the young plant and for people, too! *Where can we find seeds? There are seeds in the fruits and vegetables you eat.*

Seeds we eat: sunflower, nuts, peas, corn, coconut, grains like wheat and oats

Seeds we meet but do on eat: peach, avocado, apple, orange

Seeds on the Move

If all seeds grew where they fell, they'd have a crowding problem! Seeds have special features to help them travel for survival. Kids can write and illustrate their discoveries in a booklet they create called *Seeds on the Move.* Pages might show:

✳ Puffy dandelion seeds fly in the wind.

✳ Coconuts and cranberries float on water.

✳ Star thistle catches on animal fur.

✳ Acorns are buried by squirrels.

✳ Maple seeds spin and flutter.

✳ Berries are eaten by birds and the seeds are left somewhere else.

⚓ Seed Safari

Where do seeds come from? Once kids have "seed awareness," they'll notice them everywhere! Organize a seed safari to get them searching and thinking.

MATERIALS: large socks to fit over children's shoes, hand lens

1. Have children pull a large sock over one shoe. Take kids on a walk through a field with dried grass and weeds.

2. Back in the classroom or at home, have kids carefully pull the seeds of their socks and sort them into different piles, then examine with a hand lens. Encourage sorting by size, shape, color, special features, the child's own way. *Look closely at the different seeds. How are they the same and different? Can you guess how they hook onto your sock? Why do seeds need to get around?*

⟳DEEPEN kids' understanding

Read *Jack in the Beanstalk* or *The Tiny Seed* by Eric Carle. *Are these stories science or pretend? What makes you think so?* Have kids glue a seed near the bottom of a sheet of art paper. *What sort of plant might your seed become?* Use markers to draw a make-believe plant in rainbow colors, blooming toys, or whatever you imagine!

Making Everyday Connections

Music: Make the rattle on page 112. Fill it with beans.

Math: *Estimate the number of beans in a jar (start with about 25). Now count the beans. Was your estimate reasonable? Compare* the volume of 20 popcorn kernels in a bowl with 20 popped kernels. *Measure* the length of a sprout with yarn segments. Tape and date each segment on a sheet of cardboard.

Social Studies: Every culture has seed cuisine. Taste seed foods such as bean burritos from Central America, sesame rice from Asia, chickpea and sesame hummus dip from the Middle East.

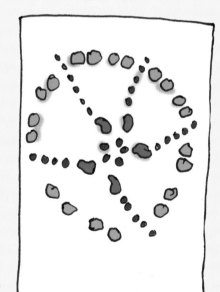

⚓ Make a Seed Masterpiece!

MATERIALS: pencil, cardboard, glue, variety of seeds (beans, grains, wild seeds)

Have kids outline a picture on a small piece of cardboard. Show how to squeeze white glue onto short segments of the outline. Press seeds in place. Fill in areas with smaller seeds.

Everywhere Science

I don't need whiz-bang experiments to turn my kids on to science. I have found the wonder in everyday experiences to be most effective. Familiar materials such as seeds, rocks, or water are prime for study because they invite firsthand investigation. Kids' developing expertise motivates them to learn on their own as they encounter these common materials in other contexts throughout their day. Once kids see the ordinary as extraordinary, recess becomes fascinating. They enthusiastically share pebbles they find on the playground or seeds from their apple at snack time. Their world is alive with science!

Social Studies

Learning about people, places, times, and interdependence

Kindergartners are naturally interested in themselves, their families and friends, and their neighborhoods. They are focused on what's happening to them today. Kindergarten Social Studies uses the familiar as a springboard to broaden children's understanding beyond their immediate community to people and places in different locations and times.

Through stories of ordinary and extraordinary people, kindergartners learn how ideals enrich our lives and strengthen our communities. They learn that as members of a greater community, they contribute to that group, and they learn to respectfully interrelate with others.

Children discover how we are all part of a common human experience shaped through time by continuity *and* change. For instance, although today's shopping mall hardly resembles a marketplace of the past, values like *liberty* (having the freedom to make choices) and *justice* (having laws that make sure everyone is treated in an equal and fair way) *for all* (for everyone!) are still core tenets of our nation.

It's Standard!

Kindergarten curriculum includes:

* Citizenship
* Community
* Geography
* History
* Patriotic symbols

I Am a Citizen, Too!

Citizenship bestows us with both rights and responsibilities. I find that
when my classroom works as a community, my students learn firsthand about
responsible citizenship. To begin, I bring values to a conscious level through discussion.
Then we put our thoughts into action by practicing values such as self-respect,
teamwork, or perseverance, kindergarten-style. Here are a few character traits of
good citizens to discuss, model by example, and guide through encouragement.
Remember to reinforce with praise whenever you catch kids in the
act of being good citizens at home or at school!

Responsibility Rules!

Discuss. *Being responsible means honoring our commitments and accepting the consequences for what we say and do.*

Model. *I said we'd go to the park after school today, so let's go!*

Guide. *Remember, I said you could have the book after you put your toys away.*

On their own. *Thanks for picking up the Legos you spilled. You are so responsible!*

Let's Be Fair

Discuss. *Fairness is acting in a way that is just and honest. It's playing by the rules so that all are treated equally. Trust, based on honesty, holds families and communities together.*

Model. *Zack can pick the story today because Sadie chose it yesterday.*

Guide. *When everyone plays by the rules, the game goes smoothly. Try it!*

On their own. *Look how long you've played the game with everyone getting along! Way to go!*

Compassion Is Kindness

Discuss. *Compassion is concern for other people's feelings and needs. It includes tolerance for other views and beliefs.*

Model. *You must feel good about tying your own shoes. Good job, Kerstin!*

Guide. *How do you think Josh feels? What can you do to make him feel better?*

On their own. *What good listeners you were while Justin told us about his family's New Year's celebration!*

Make "Good Citizenship" Medals

Catch kids in the act of being good citizens. Honor their efforts!

MATERIALS: yarn, old CD, scissors, paper, markers or crayons, glue

1. Loop a yard of yarn through the center of an old CD.

2. Cut a circle of paper to cover the print side of the CD.

3. Help children write *I am compassionate* (or *responsible, fair, honest . . .*) along the edge. Have children illustrate their acts of citizenship.

4. Glue the paper circle to the CD.

5. Proudly wear your medal! In a classroom, illustrate and display acts of citizenship all around the room.

Making Everyday Connections

Stories have long been a powerful tool for teaching values to children. Focus on the characters' values and the author's message. I strengthen the message in my classroom by relating children's behavior to the story: *Great teamwork, kids! Just like the folks in* **The Enormous Turnip** *folktale.*

As an added bonus, we practice the comprehension strategy of making connections (see Strategy Savvy, page 34).

Fables. And the moral of the story is . . . *How did the slow tortoise win over the speedy hare? Why should a lion be kind to a mouse?*

Folktales. *Was Goldilocks good? Why or why not? What can we learn from the story of* **The Three Little Pigs**?

Historical accounts. Libraries and bookstores abound with picture books about heroes and extraordinary people. Guide kids to discover the courage of Susan B. Anthony and the leadership of Dr. Martin Luther King Jr.

DEEPEN kids' understanding

Help children grapple with the values displayed in stories, television programs, and real life with guided questions:

✳ *Were the characters trying to be helpful or hurtful? Were they thinking of others?*

✳ *Who were the heroes (good guys)? Who were the villains (bad guys)?*

✳ *Did people make good choices? How did they deal with hard times?*

✳ *How could there have been a happy ending for everyone?*

Encourage kids to think aloud by adding: *Why or why not? What makes you think so?*

Community Helpers

What makes a community? People working together to make things better for everyone! Firefighters, teachers, police officers, construction workers, office workers, and so many others are the everyday heroes who strengthen our communities. Guide kindergartners in discovering how these helpers keep us safe, smart, healthy, and happy. And remind them, they can be community helpers making a difference, too!

 ## Getting to Know You!

MATERIALS: tape recorder or clipboard and paper, markers

Encourage kids to interview their family members and other community helpers, then draw or write about what they learn. Guide kids through the interview process with some sample questions:

✳ What is your job?

✳ Where do you work?

✳ What special skills must you know how to do?

✳ What special tools do you need?

✳ What do you like and dislike about your job?

✳ Why are you proud of your work?

⚓Try On a Job!

Pretend play is a great way for kids to "try on" roles in the workplace. Add key props to transform a playhouse into a business, doctor's office, or fire station. Kids naturally interact as if they are business owners, clients, or service personnel when they are inspired by the setting (see PRETEND WITH PRINT!, page 16, for more ideas).

Kids can also create their own mini-stages to act out grown-up roles after reading picture books or talking with community helpers.

MATERIALS: small photo of the child's face (about 1"/2.5 cm in diameter, such as a small school photo), paste, index card, markers, scissors, tape, drinking straw, paper, large paper clips, cereal box

1. ***Make the "What I'll Be" puppet.*** Paste each child's photo near the top of an index card. Invite children to use markers to add the clothing and headgear they'll need to wear. Cut the image out. Tape a drinking straw to the top back of each puppet.

2. ***Create a workplace stage.*** Have kids draw their puppet's workplace on a sheet of paper. Clip the paper to the open top edge of a cereal box.

3. ***Off to work!*** Each child takes a turn telling about a day at work, using her puppet and stage.

DEEPEN kids' understanding

Practice *inferential thinking* by playing a guessing game!

🕴 Who Am I?

Give three clues about a job. Let kids ask yes or no questions until they think they know the answer and are ready to guess. *I spend time in the sky. I help people get from here to there. I always need to pay attention. Who am I?* "A pilot!" Take turns so that everyone gets a try at being the "worker."

Making Everyday Connections

So many of my kindergartners are convinced they'll be a princess or rock star when they grow up. They often don't realize that their fascinating interests can become careers. I like to let them know there are MANY options.

Language Arts: author, publisher, journalist, librarian

Arts: illustrator, Web designer, musician, actor, dancer

Construction: engineer, construction worker, architect

Mathematics: electrical engineer, computer scientist, aerospace engineer

Science: biologist, doctor, geologist, veterinarian, oceanographer

Food: cook, farmer, baker, pizza-shop owner

Once kids "decide" on career goals with the help of their parents, I reinforce their choice: *Awesome job counting, Emma. You can be an aerospace engineer!*

Where in the World?

Grab your jacket. It's another windy day!

I wonder why so many oak trees grow here?

The map shows that a right turn on Hilltop Road is the best way to get to Kaitlyn's house.

Comments such as these help children learn about *geography* —
an awareness of the nature of the earth and their place on it. Kindergartners
discover what makes a place special, where landmarks and physical features are
located, and the interconnections people and wildlife have to the places they live.

⚓ My Favorite Place

MATERIALS: postcards and travel brochures
about your town or area, large index cards,
markers or crayons, ruler (optional),
postage stamps

1. ***Look at*** postcards and travel brochures
   about your town and the surrounding
   area. ***Ask questions to guide the***
   thinking such as *What makes the*
   Lakeside Arboretum so special? What do
   you like best about Discovery Museum?

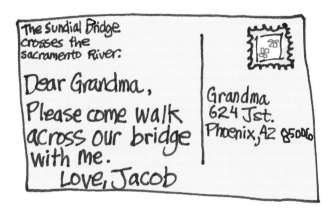

The Sundial Bridge crosses the Sacramento River:

Dear Grandma,
Please come walk across our bridge with me.
Love, Jacob

Grandma
624 J st.
Phoenix, AZ 85006

2. **Make a picture postcard:** Have children draw a picture of a favorite place on one side of a large index card. Flip the card over. Help them draw a line down the center and write a brief description in the top left corner.

3. **Extend the experience:** Invite kids to write (or scribe for them) a message to a faraway friend on their picture postcard. Add stamps and mail it off. *What are some ways ideas travel from place to place?*

👤 Make a
TRAVEL BROCHURE!

Tri-fold a sheet of paper for a child to create a travel brochure of his town. Or, in a classroom, have each child draw and write about his special place on a sheet of paper. Assemble as a travel book entitled *Welcome to [Your town], U.S.A.!*

Welcome to Oakville USA

Map It!

Maps make a picture of real geographic features and man-made landscapes. Build this fascinating concept by encouraging kids to make models of landforms and city features through sand and block play. Young children can also learn to read simple diagrams of their homes, school grounds, and neighborhoods. Help them develop concepts of scale, perspective, and symbols as they map it, themselves!

My Room. The simplest map to make is one where all points you wish to map are visible. Have kids sit with a sheet of paper and clipboard in their bedroom, classroom, or playground. Draw what they see, placing each object in relation to the next.

With so much curricular focus on reading, writing, and arithmetic, students with other strengths often don't get to shine. I find that mapping brings out the talents of my visual thinkers. Hello, future geo-spatial experts!

My Town. Map a favorite part of town to show landforms, bodies of water, or key structures such as libraries, markets, schools, or parks. Then, use the map to get from here to there! Most kids know the route from home to school. Captivate them with a real map of the route.

Making Everyday Connections

Build map awareness throughout the day and in play.

Share local maps. Let kids "navigate" as you drive. Kids will discover firsthand that maps are a valuable tool and how to use them. Highlight where you go on a map to show your route on a trip.

Use diagrams for museums and other sites when touring. *Let's see, we want to get to the Animal Exhibit. How shall we get there? Let's use the museum map to find our way.*

Refer to a globe when countries are mentioned in the news or stories.

Play board games, such as Candy Land, that map a journey. Assemble world, country, or state puzzles together (there are even city puzzles that show the landmarks of the local area).

Map storybook adventures of characters such as the Three Billy Goats Gruff or the Gingerbread Man.

Search the Internet for aerial photography. Visit **terraserver.com** for a sky-high views of places on earth.

Take a map view. From an upstairs window, or from a high floor of a building, point out how the world below looks small, like a map.

Home on the Land

How do people adjust to their place on the earth? The Native Americans who lived in North America long ago were so resourceful! They used the natural materials around them such as the skins of animals, the bark and branches from trees, and soil and grasses to create dwellings that respected nature. *Pretend you are living long ago. What could you use from the land to build your home?*

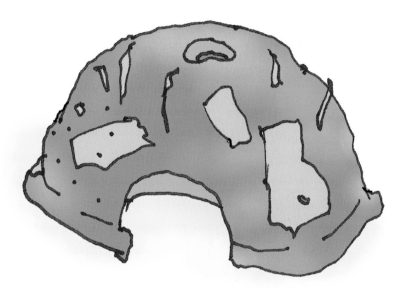

 ## Brickworks

Native Americans and pioneers built homes of adobe brick. Let kids experience creating building materials right from their yards. Have them hand-blend a mixture of soil, grass clippings, and water. Press into an ice cube tray for mini-bricks or the bottom half of a half-gallon milk carton for larger bricks. Remove when completely dry after several days.

 ## Home, Sweet Home

Have kids build a miniature home using materials found in their own backyards.

MATERIALS
* 2 small bowls
* Plastic bag
* 1 cup (250 ml) fine dirt
* 1/2 cup (125 ml) flour
* Water
* Grass, small leaves, twigs
* Scraps of brown paper bag

1. Wrap one bowl in the plastic bag. Set it upside down.

2. In the other bowl, mix the dirt with the flour. Add enough water to make clay. Press the mixture on the outside of the plastic-covered bowl, leaving an entrance opening and a smoke hole in the roof.

3. Press grass, small leaves, and twigs into the mud. Wet the scraps of the paper bag. Press them into the mud to look like animal hides.

4. When the house is completely dry, carefully lift it off the bowl.

DEEPEN kids' understanding

Geographic understanding includes *interdependence of peoples and places* around the world. Help children see how people, products, and ideas are on the move. Include animal connections, too!

Notice labels on clothing and food. Think about television images, music, art, or mail. *Where does it come from? Let's find the locations on a globe.*

Check the license plates of trucks on the road during a trip. *Where do they drive from? What do you think they carry?*

Offer a global view. Talk with folks who were born in or have visited other countries. Have them compare children's lives in distant lands with local children's lives.

Hunt for animal shelters in parks and natural areas where you live. Challenge children to consider what materials a bird uses to build a nest, wasps use to create their hive, or beavers use to build their lodge. *Why do you think they build this way?*

It's History!

Kindergartners may not realize it, but they were born into history. Their lives and events create the continuous story everyone, past and present, is part of. Through people and their stories — of their struggles, traditions, ideas, and ideals — today's world is connected to worlds of long ago. History begins at home and at school with memories passed from one generation to the next, and from class to class.

⚓ Tradition Keeper

Traditions are what people do in a special way every year, like having picnics on the Fourth of July or eating moon cake at New Year's. Foods, songs, games, celebrations . . . anything we do can become a tradition.

Help children realize that traditions from the *past* and can be enjoyed *today*, then shared with their own children who will live in the *future* by creating a special TRADITION KEEPER that will store those special recipes, games, celebrations, and ways of doing things so they will always be remembered.

MATERIALS: 2 paper plates, scissors, hole punch, markers, 2 yards (2 m) yarn, index cards

1. Cut plates into matching heart shapes. Punch matching holes around the bottom edge of both plates.

2. Have children decorate the hearts with markers and add their family name (or classroom number).

3. Have children stitch the hearts together. Tie the ends of the yarn into a bow for hanging.

4. Children write or draw a favorite family tradition on index cards, one for each tradition. Store the cards in the keeper.

Families can decide which traditions to include:

We light lamps for Diwali. We hike Mount Shasta every July 4th.

Recipe for Grandma's cabbage rolls

Classroom traditions might include:

We pick a Student of the Month.

We celebrate the 100th day of school.

Lyrics to our favorite song

Making Everyday Connections

History is the toys kids play with, what they watched on TV last night, and what ideas are important to them right now. Help kids realize their lives today, this minute, will be history!

Think Like an Archaeologist

Guide brainstorming about what our artifacts tell about us. _Pretend you find items from today one hundred years from now. What will these things tell you about how people lived "long ago"?_

Candy wrapper, soda can, chicken bone. _How did these people eat?_

CD, broken toy, computer. _What did these people do for fun?_

Roller skates, car tire, bus ticket. _How did they travel?_

 Our Story

Create a binder of family history. Kids can draw, scribe, or write about an important event as it happens. Be sure to date each page. _January 7, 2005. My sister Kate was born. I became a big brother._ Invite visiting relatives to add pages that precede your child's life. Have your child help you place pages in chronological order.

In a classroom, keep a binder of important events throughout the year. Have different kids volunteer to make the entry for the first day, the 100th day, field trips, assemblies, and memorable learning units. Invite school personnel to make entries about important past events such as when the school opened or when the playground was built.

Holidays Are History Days

National holidays bring people together to remember great events and people in history. We fly the flag, share a feast, visit a memorial, or watch a parade to show respect for the values that define our country.

Martin Luther King Jr. Day

Young children appreciate justice. "That's not fair!" is as much a child's frustration as it is an adult's. Dr. Martin Luther King Jr. taught Americans that the powerful words of the Declaration of Independence, "all men are created equal," are true for *all* people, no matter what their skin color. He taught through peaceful marches and powerful speeches that even if we look different from one another, we must still respect each other. Because of his leadership, laws were changed to protect the rights of all Americans.

January 15 is Dr. King's birthday. On the third Monday in January every year, we honor his work for peace and equal rights for all.

My kindergartners are very touched by Dr. King's story. We hold hands while listening to the song "A Man Named King" on *Greg and Steve's Holiday's and Special Times* CD. Lots of hugs spontaneously follow. We brainstorm ways to keep Dr. King's dream alive. It always comes down to respecting one another!

Make a Brotherhood Wreath

MATERIALS: scissors, large paper plate, cup, construction paper, yarn, markers, glue, streamers (red, white, and blue)

1. Cut the center from a large paper plate, leaving a 2" (5 cm) rim.

2. Use a 3" diameter (7.5 cm) cup as a template for making face circles. Cut the circles from a different skin-tone shades (black, brown, tan, white) of construction paper.

3. Have children decorate circles to make mini self-portraits, using paper scraps, yarn, and markers to add hair, face details, and headgear.

4. Glue the faces around the edge of the plate. Add red, white, and blue streamers at the bottom. Hang as a wreath.

In our kindergarten class, each child makes her own face and name label, and adds it to a classroom wreath.

The Big Idea

Help children understand Dr. King's message: "I have a dream that my four little children will one day live in a nation where they will not be judged by the color of their skin but by the content of their character."

✳ *What makes a good person? A good friend?*

✳ *How do you decide if someone will be your friend?*

✳ *Draw a picture to show how you can keep Dr. King's dream alive.*

⟲DEEPEN kids' understanding

I used to think I'd "covered" Thanksgiving by sending my students home with a cute turkey craft. Now, a central theme runs through my curriculum that inspires my students to look for the "big ideas" behind important events and heroes. After studying a holiday, I ask, *So what does it mean to be an American?*

Independence Day (celebrated on July 4). *Ordinary people decided to rule themselves. On the Fourth of July, we celebrate the "birthday" of America!*

Presidents' Day (celebrated on the third Monday in February): *We honor all past presidents, but especially George Washington and Abraham Lincoln. These men made decisions that kept the country joined as the **United** States of America.*

Labor Day (celebrated on the first Monday in September): *We honor all the hardworking community helpers who keep us safe, smart, healthy, and happy.*

Celebrate Red, White, and Blue

Symbols are nifty because something simple (a heart shape) can stand for something complex (love). Kindergartners encounter the number one symbol of our country, the American flag, on the first day of school!

Me and My Flag

Kids can make a flag that says, "I'm proud to be an American!"

MATERIALS

✳ Markers

✳ 4½" x 6" (11 x 15 cm) rectangle of blue paper

✳ Adhesive stars (optional)

✳ Glue

✳ Strips of red paper to form the stripes: 4 short strips, ½" x 5" (1 x 12.5 cm), and 3 longer strips, ½" x 11" (1 x 27.5 cm)

✳ Sheet of 8½" x 11" (21 x 27.5 cm) white paper

✳ Brown paper grocery bag

✳ Scissors

✳ Drinking straw

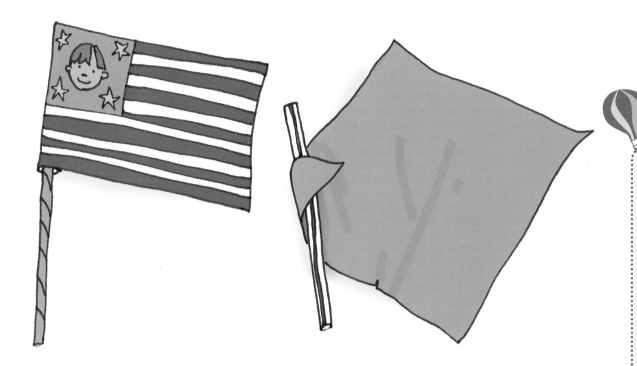

1. Kids use markers to draw themselves on the blue rectangle. Stick on some stars if desired.

2. Glue the blue rectangle and the red stripes onto the white paper as shown.

3. Together, make the stick handle: Cut the front from a grocery bag. Starting from one corner, roll all the paper onto the straw. Glue the edge to hold it together.

4. Glue the handle to the back of the flag.

Making Everyday Connections

Help kids notice flags and other patriotic symbols throughout the day. Flags are displayed on many buildings; patriotic symbols appear in advertising. Take a close look at coins, and talk about the eagles, monuments, and people they see pictured. Let kids make coin rubbings to capture the symbols. *What symbols say "America" to you?*

The Arts

Creating with motion, music, and materials

Young children are bold artists. They don't hesitate to bang out a beat or thickly brush on bright paint. Dramatic play happens even without an audience, and dance is just another way of getting from here to there. The challenge in kindergarten is to offer new possibilities without diminishing the child's confident, creative spirit!

It's Standard!

In kindergarten, children not only *create* art, they learn to *appreciate* art as they explore four core disciplines:

* Dance
* Music
* Drama
* Visual Arts

Got to Dance!

Dance is a universal language children readily speak. Dancers communicate by moving through space; so do children. Kids don't merely walk — they wiggle, tiptoe, skip, and crawl! Exploring dance brings movement to a conscious level. Children learn they can use their own bodies for extraordinary communication. Here are some ways to inspire imaginative movement.

Watch Me Move!

I am a ... Imagine you are a tree (or the sun, a rainbow, a river, a mountain, or thunder!). *How would you act if you could move?*

Mood Moves. *Move as if you are happy (angry, tired, sad, excited, lost, hot, freezing).*

Thingamajig. Invite kids to use props — a streamer, scarf, or rattle — in their dances.

Create a Body Shape. *Walk with it. Glide with it. Jump with it. Fly with it.*

⚓ Partner Play

Machine. Two or more kids make a machine in which each child is a part, repeating a movement. Another child turns the machine on or off, speeds it up, or slows it down.

Mirror. Partners face each other. One child leads by moving, and the other child mirrors the movement. Then have children reverse roles.

Sculpture. One child is clay; the other is a sculptor, molding the clay into a shape. The sculptor steps away and admires the sculpture, then children reverse roles.

Catch. Kids play catch with an imaginary ball or Frisbee.

DEEPEN kids' understanding

Invite children to be critics. Have children think about their own movements and dances of their friends. *What makes a dance interesting to watch? How do props change your movement? Which is your favorite way to dance — with a partner or alone?*

Build the vocabulary of dance: **backward/forward, move/freeze, bold/timid; turn, stretch, reach, skip, drop, slide, roll, hop, gallop, twist!**

Making Everyday Connections

Foster links between dance, music, and drama. Have children try these dance activities to a variety of music genres: folk, jazz, classical, new age. *How do your movements change with the different moods of the music?*

Encourage children to dance what they learn from topics of study. For example, after my students study the life cycle of a butterfly, I play classical music and say, *Hatch from an egg, wiggle like a caterpillar, spin a cocoon, and emerge as a beautiful butterfly.* The children love it! I find that having them express information through a new medium cements learning.

Let's Make Music!

Young children are natural musicians. Their energetic bodies clap, stomp, and boogie to a beat. Singing and humming are the background music of their play.

A successful kindergarten embraces this innate musicianship by exploring the possibilities of music-making. And since the best way to understand music is to start making it, get kids clapping, snapping, humming, and strumming throughout the day!

Shake Rattle & Roll!

These homemade band instruments are simple enough for young children to make almost on their own.

Assign instruments to different groups of children. Kids can play to the beat of music on a CD or a song they sing. A conductor can lead the band by pointing to each group with her chopstick baton.

Rattle

MATERIALS: toilet-paper tube, markers or tempera paints and brush, stapler, rice or beans, paper streamers

1. Have children decorate the toilet-paper tube with markers or paint. Pinch one end and staple it closed.

2. Kids can add a handful of beans or rice to the tube. Then pinch the other end perpendicular to the stapled end. Help kids insert paper streamers, then staple closed.

Drum

MATERIALS: coffee cans or oatmeal containers, paper, markers or tempera paints and brush, glue or paste

Coffee cans and oatmeal boxes make perfect drums. Help children cover the sides by gluing on kid-decorated paper. Tap the lid with fingertips.

 Box Guitar

MATERIALS: tissue box, rubber bands of different sizes

Kids can stretch rubber bands of various thicknesses across the opening of a tissue box. Now pluck and strum!

Kazoo

MATERIALS: hole punch, toilet-paper tube, markers, rubber band, waxed paper

1. Punch a hole about 1.5" (3.5 cm) from the top of a toilet-paper tube.

2. Have kids decorate the tube with markers.

3. Use a rubber band to hold a circle of waxed paper in place just above the punched hole. Hum into the open end.

Sing a Song

Even the most musically challenged grownup can model great singing. Just turn on a CD! Kids can sing along with the best, from Raffi to Disney to dozens of lesser-known artists.

Be a songwriter! My kindergartners love to make up their own songs by "piggybacking" on the classics. For example, we've used "Here We Go 'Round the Mulberry Bush" to reinforce behavior (*This is the way ... we share our toys*), learn science (*... a turtle moves, a nest is built*), or just have fun (*... we build with blocks*).

Children can write the words and draw a picture of a verse they create about themselves from the piggyback songs. In a classroom, these can be assembled as pages for a book of original lyrics!

Making Everyday Connections

Literacy: Use music to build understanding of the sounds within words (phonemic awareness, page 22).

Math: Have kids clap, snap, and stomp math patterns described on page 45.

Social Studies: Teach historic songs such as "Yankee Doodle" or "She'll Be Coming 'Round the Mountain." Talk about patriotic songs such as "This Land Is My Land" or "God Bless America." Share world music with young listeners.

Science: Set facts to music to cement learning. *Sing this verse with me to the tune of "The Farmer in the Dell": The roots support the tree. The roots support the tree. They're deep and wide beneath the ground. The roots support the tree.*

Art: Invite kids to use a marker to make an enormous squiggle inspired by music. Continue to play the music as they color in the shapes they made with crayons or watercolors.

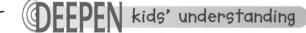 **DEEPEN** kids' understanding

Build communication skills by talking about great music. There are no right answers, just pondering and imagining. After listening to a piece, ask a few questions to get kids thinking:

✳ *What do you hear in the music?*

✳ *How does the music make you feel?*

✳ *What does the music remind you of?*

✳ *What do you imagine while you listen?*

✳ *What might the composer be trying to say?*

Follow each question with: *What makes you think so?*

Get into the Act!

Kindergarten drama is a rehearsal for life. Drama sets the stage for developing imagination, solving problems, building communication skills, and understanding interactions with others. Drama can happen spontaneously, inspired by the props in a play center. Or, kindergartners might receive explicit acting instruction while preparing for a class performance. Make drama part of the daily routine, from a dramatic read-aloud of a story to the "vroom" of cars darting about the block center!

⚓ Pantomime Fun

Everyday actions are fun to act out without words. Prompt kids to take turns acting out familiar scenarios (eating a banana, playing ball, trying to walk on slippery ice, swatting at a mosquito) while the others guess the action. *What movements could we add to make it seem more real?*

Stories Alive!

Children love to act out a favorite story while a grown-up leader narrates the tale. Assign roles. Have kids make safe headgear for their characters with simple household materials. Then pass out a few simple props and let the play begin!

 ## Make a Top-Hat Mask

MATERIALS: scissors, paper grocery bag, markers, paint and paintbrush, crayons, newspaper and colored paper scraps, glue, stapler

1. Cut open a paper grocery bag. Fit it to the child's head, cutting the bag to size as needed.

2. Have kids use markers, paints, or crayons to create the character's face in the center.

3. Add details, like fringed newspaper strips for hair or a pop-out nose and ears.

4. Staple the bag to fit around the actor's head.

Puppet Play

I find some of my students are more comfortable performing through a puppet than on their own. Shy kids instantly become stars with a puppet on their hands. Provide store-bought puppets, or better yet, use children's creations. Classic paper-bag puppets are wonderful because kindergartners can make them on their own. Provide paper scraps, markers, and crayons. Show how the mouth will work.

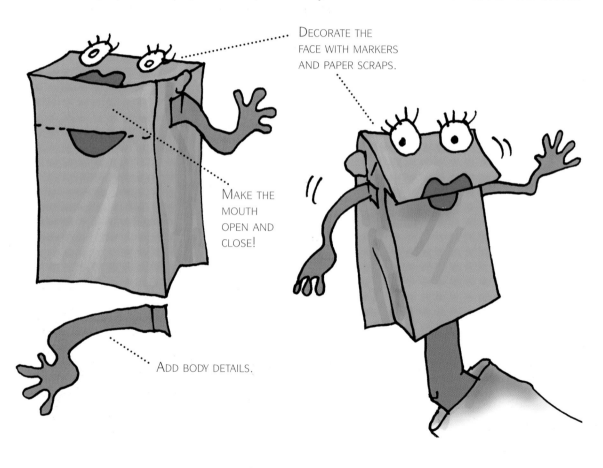

DECORATE THE FACE WITH MARKERS AND PAPER SCRAPS.

MAKE THE MOUTH OPEN AND CLOSE!

ADD BODY DETAILS.

Stick Puppets

Children can also make simple stick puppets and a simple stage for creating their own backdrop (see page 94). This is a hands-on way to teach *characters* and *setting*. With puppets in hand, children spontaneously retell and dramatize stories they've heard read aloud, or create their own.

◎DEEPEN *kids' understanding*

Info Act. Just as children act out stories they've heard read aloud, they can also act out what they learn from informational text. Turn on neutral background music. Retell facts in a story style while the children act out your words.

You are an acorn lying beneath an oak tree. Suddenly a squirrel buries you beneath the ground. It is dark. You are all alone. Listen. There is pounding above. Now you feel wet. The wetter you get, the fatter you get. You burst out of your seed coat. Now you feel roots growing beneath you. You begin to sprout through the earth . . . Wow! Sunshine and air. Your tiny leaves begin to make food. . .

Role Play. Skits provide a safe platform for problem-solving how to best get along with others. Have kids create a skit showing contrasting problematic and successful behaviors. The audience can judge which way results in a safe, happy home or classroom. Sample topics include: putting toys away, taking turns, bedtime routine, sharing.

Theater Speak. Describe experiences with vocabulary in the language of theater: **actor, director, audience, stage, set, character, backdrop, prop, costume, pantomime, puppet, mask**

Art Start

Creative expression happens when art is a *process*. Kindergarten art best reflects children's ideas and feelings if projects are open-ended. Empower children with generic techniques for creating their own visions. Share art from other times and places to build appreciation for those cultures and fuel the child's imagination for what is possible.

Paper Play

Show kids the creative potential of a humble sheet of paper. It's safe, readily available, and so versatile!

 ### Cut and Paste Matisse-Style

Elevate cut-and-paste fun to the masterpiece level. Look at Matisse cutouts such as *Ivy in Flower* or *Icarus*. Notice the mix of shapes: ovals, spirals, stars, natural shapes, and more. Set out sheets of astro-bright paper. Encourage kids to cut out shapes of their own inspired by Matisse. Try different arrangements on white paper. Let kids paste the shapes in place when they are pleased with their layouts.

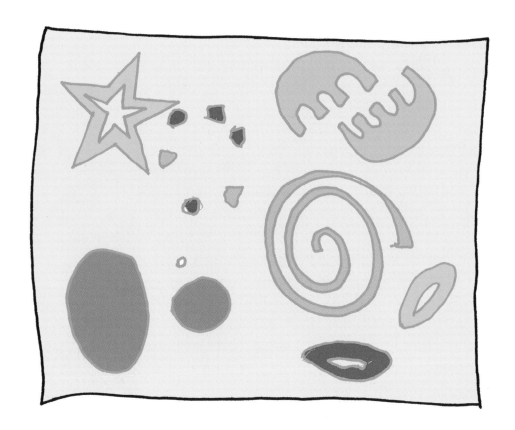

Make Papal Picado

Children love the magic of snipping multifolded paper to produce repeating symmetrical (mirror image) shapes. Kindergartners can apply this technique to make their own versions of Papal Picado (pierced paper). Mexican children create this fold craft for celebrations.

MATERIALS: sheet of lightweight paper, scissors, string, tape or glue

1. Kids fold a sheet of paper in half, twice.

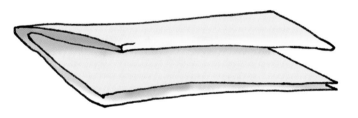

2. Snip small shapes from the edges. (Do not cut from edge to edge or the paper will fall apart.) Unfold the paper to see the pattern.

3. Fold the top edge over a string. Tape or glue down the edge.

4. Make many more and glue onto the string to make a longer banner.

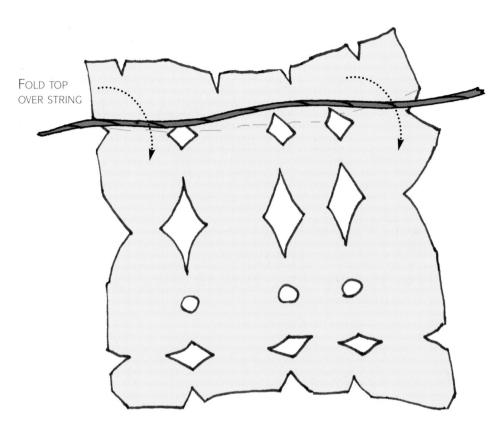

FOLD TOP OVER STRING

MORE **FUN!**

❋ *Rainbow banner.* Use colors of paper in this order: red, orange, yellow, green, blue, indigo, violet.

❋ *Cinco de Mayo* (a victory celebration) *banner.* Use the colors of the Mexican flag: red, white, and green.

❋ *Fourth of July banner.* Use red, white, and blue.

 **Make a Pop-Up Card**

The back-and-forth accordion fold is one of the simplest paper techniques of all!
Show kids how to use it to make a fan or the bouncy legs of a crazy paper critter. We use the
fold to add interest to greeting cards. Explain how to fold paper in half and draw a picture on
the front. Then add a message and a surprise inside with an accordion-folded paper strip!

MATERIALS: colored paper, markers, scissors, glue

1. Fold the paper in half to make a card. Draw a picture on the front.

2. Cut a thin (1" x 4"/2.5 x 10 cm) strip of paper for a spring mechanism. Glue one end to the inside of the card. Glue a small cut-out picture or paper decoration on the other end.

3. Open the card . . . surprise!

My kindergartners love creating and giving greeting cards to friends. It's a great way for them to connect art to literacy. I create a greeting-card center at birthdays and other holidays by simply setting out sample commercial cards for these occasions plus art and writing supplies. Of course, a friendship card is welcome anytime!

DEEPEN kids' understanding

Encouraging kindergartners to observe, reflect, and communicate their ideas develops the powerful thinking skills they'll need for success throughout school and beyond. When sharing masterpieces at a museum or in a book with children, get the conversation going about art with a questions such as these:

✳ *What's happening in the painting (sculpture, print)?*

✳ *What colors and shapes do you recognize?*

✳ *Does it look like something you know?*

✳ *What might have happened before the scene?*

✳ *What might happen next?*

✳ *What do you think the artist might be telling us?*

Making Everyday Connections

Because so much of young children's written communication is drawing, kindergartners are artists throughout the day. Encourage art connections across the curriculum.

Math: Cut and paste patterns. Draw pictures of word problems.

Science: Draw observations. Make labeled drawing of plants and animals.

Literacy: Have children illustrate their own mini-books. They can draw what they visualize while a story is being read aloud.

Resources

Research

Preventing Reading Difficulties in Young Children by the Committee on the Prevention of Reading Difficulties in Young Children, National Research Council; <nap.edu>

Teaching Children to Read
Putting Reading First
by the National Reading Panel; <nationalreadingpanel.org>

State Standards Links

<edstandards.org/Standards.html>

Literacy Websites

Between the Lions; <pbs.org/kids> and <ctw.org>
Learn-to-read PBS television program with support website.

starfall.com
headsprout.com
Web-based phonics programs.

Learning Manipulatives

<**Lakeshore**learning.com>
<**Etacuisenaire**.com>
<**Readingmanipulatives**.com>
<**Childcraft**.com>

Science Materials

<**InsectLore**.com>
Biological resources

<**SteveSpanglerScience**.com>
Physical Science resources

<lhsgems.org>
GEMS (Great Explorations in Math and Science)

Alphabet Books

Alphabatics by Suse MacDonald
Q is for Duck: An Alphabet Guessing Game by Mary Elting & Michael Folsom
Tomorrow's Alphabet by George Shannon
Alphabet City by Stephen T. Johnson

Books for Beginners

<**Sundance**pub.com>
<**Rigby**.com>
<**Scholastic**.com>
<**Hampton-Brown**.com>
<**WrightGroup**.com>

Celebrate Literacy

Click, Clack, Moo: Cows That Type and *Diary of a Worm* by Doreen Cronin
The Jolly Postman by Janet and Allan Ahlberg
Never Let Your Cat Make Lunch for You by Lee Harris
Bunny Cakes by Rosemary Wells
Love, Your Bear Pete by Dylan Sheldon
I Like Books by Anthony Browne

Great Stories for Comprehension

David and Dog by Shirley Hughes
Alexander and the Wind-Up Mouse and *Swimmy* by Leo Lionni
Sylvester and the Magic Pebble and *Doctor De Soto* by William Steig

Informational Text

Let's-Read-and-Find-Out-Science Series (HarperTrophy)
Backyard Books (Kingfisher)
Let's Try it Out, Hello Reader-Science, A Picture Book Biographies (Scholastic)
DK Readers (Dorling Kindersley)

Phonemic Awareness/Phonics

Pat the Cat and Friends by Colin Hawkins
Fun with Phonics by Sue Graves
Where's My Teddy, It's the Bear, and *My Friend Bear* by Jez Alborough
Saturday Night at the Dinosaur Stomp by Carol Shields

Index

More Good Books from Williamson

Welcome to Williamson Books! Our books are available from your bookseller or directly from Williamson Books at Ideals Publications. Please see the next page for ordering information or to visit our website. Thank you.

All books are suitable for children ages 3 through 7, and are 120 to 128 pages,10 x 8, $12.95, unless otherwise noted.

More Award-Winning Books by Jill Hauser!

Parents' Choice Recommended
EASY ART FUN!
Do-It-Yourself Crafts for Beginning Readers
A *Little Hands*® Read-&-Do book

American Institute of Physics Science Writing Award
Parents' Choice Honor Award
American Bookseller Pick of the Lists
Benjamin Franklin Best Education/Teaching Book Award
GIZMOS & GADGETS
Creating Science Contraptions that Work (& Knowing Why)
A Williamson *Kids Can!*® book for ages 7 to 14, 144 pages, 11 x 8½

American Bookseller Pick of the Lists
Dr. Toy Best Vacation Product
KIDS' CRAZY ART CONCOCTIONS
50 Mysterious Mixtures for Art & Craft Fun
A Williamson *Kids Can!*® book for ages 7 to 14, 160 pages, 11 x 8½

Little Hands® CELEBRATE AMERICA!
Learning about the U.S.A. through Crafts & Activities

Early Childhood News Directors' Choice Award
Parents' Choice Approved
American Institute of Physics Science Writing Award
SCIENCE PLAY!
Beginning Discoveries for 2- to 6-Year-Olds

Benjamin Franklin Best Juvenile Nonfiction Award
Learning® Magazine Teachers' Choice Award
Oppenheim Toy Portfolio Best Book Award
SUPER SCIENCE CONCOCTIONS
50 Mysterious Mixtures for Fabulous Fun
A Williamson *Kids Can!*® book for ages 7 to 14, 160 pages, 11 x 8½

WOW! I'M READING!
Fun Activities to Make Reading Happen

HANDS AROUND THE WORLD
365 Creative Ways to Build Cultural Awareness & Global Respect
by Susan Milord
A Williamson *Kids Can!*® book for ages 7 to 14, 160 pages, 11 x 8½

ANIMAL HABITATS!
Learning about North American Animals & Plants through Art, Science & Creative Play
by Judy Press, full color

Parents' Choice Gold Award
FUN WITH MY 5 SENSES
Activities to Build Learning Readiness
by Sarah A. Williamson

Parents' Choice Approved
Little Hands® FINGERPLAYS & ACTION SONGS
Seasonal Rhymes & Creative Play for 2- to 6-Year-Olds
by Emily Stetson & Vicky Congdon

Parents' Choice Recommended
EARLY LEARNING SKILL-BUILDERS
Colors, Shapes, Numbers & Letters
by Mary Tomczyk

Parent's Guide Children's Media Award
ALPHABET ART
With A to Z Animal Art & Fingerplays
by Judy Press

Parents' Choice Approved
PAPER PLATE CRAFTS
Creative Art Fun for 3- to 7-year-olds
by Laura Check

ART STARTS for Little Hands!
Fun Discoveries for 3- to 7-Year-Olds
by Judy Press

Teachers' Choice Family Award
Parents' Choice Recommended
Little Hands® SEA LIFE ART & ACTIVITIES
Creative Experiences for 3- to 7-year-olds
by Judy Press

For dinosaur lovers of all ages!
IN THE DAYS OF DINOSAURS
A Rhyming Romp Through Dino History
by Howard Temperley
A Williamson *Tales Alive!*® book, all ages,
64 pages, $9.95
Full color, 8¹/₂ x 11

Parents' Choice Gold Award
Benjamin Franklin Best Juvenile Nonfiction Award
KIDS MAKE MUSIC!
Clapping and Tapping from Bach to Rock
by Avery Hart and Paul Mantell
A Williamson *Kids Can!*® book for ages
7 to 14, 160 pages, 11 x 8¹/₂

Parents' Choice Approved
The Little Hands BIG FUN CRAFT BOOK
Creative Fun for 2- to 6-Year-Olds
by Judy Press

Selection of Book-of-the-Month;
Scholastic Book Clubs
KIDS COOK!
Fabulous Food for the Whole Family
by Sarah Williamson and Zachary Williamson
A Williamson *Kids Can!*® book for ages
7 to 14, 160 pages, 11 x 8¹/₂

Parents' Choice Approved
LITTLE HANDS CREATE!
Art & Activities for Kids Ages 3 to 6
by Mary Dall

Parents' Choice Approved
GREAT GAMES!
Old & New, Indoor/Outdoor, Travel, Board, Ball & Word
by Sam Taggar
A Williamson *Kids Can!*® book for
ages 7 to 14, 11 x 8¹/₂

ForeWord Magazine Children's Book of the
Year Finalist
ALL AROUND TOWN
Exploring Your Community Through Craft Fun
by Judy Press

Parents' Choice Recommended
AT THE ZOO!
Explore the Animal World with Craft Fun
by Judy Press

WORDPLAY CAFÉ
Cool Codes, Priceless Punzles® & Phantastic Phonetic Phun
Written and illustrated by Michael Kline
A Williamson *Kids Can!*® book for ages
7 to 14, full color, 11 x 8¹/₂

AROUND-THE-WORLD ART & ACTIVITIES
Visiting the 7 Continents through Craft Fun
by Judy Press

The Little Hands PLAYTIME! BOOK
50 Activities to Encourage Cooperation & Sharing
by Regina Curtis

Visit Our Website!

To see what's new at Williamson and
learn more about specific books,
visit our secure website at:
www.williamsonbooks.com
or www.Idealsbooks.com

3 Easy Ways to Order Books:
Please visit our secure website to place
your order.
Toll-free phone orders: **1-800-586-2572**
Toll-free fax orders: **1-888-815-2759**
All major credit cards accepted (please
include the number and expiration date).

Or, send a check with your order to:
Williamson Books
Orders, Dept B.O.B.
535 Metroplex Drive, Suite 250
Nashville, TN 37211

For large volume orders or retail orders,
please call Lee Ann Bretz at
1-800-586-2572
Catalog request: mail, phone, or fax
above numbers.

Please add **$4.00** for postage for one
book plus **$1.00** for each additional
book. Satisfaction is guaranteed or full
refund without questions or quibbles.